BAC One-Eleven

KEY
Books

Front cover image: Two Braniff International Airlines stewardesses bring a touch of glamour to Bournemouth's Hurn Airport to mark the handover to the airline of its first BAC One-Eleven. In October 1961, nearly two years before the first flight of the prototype, Braniff became the first foreign customer for Britain's 'bus-stop jet' when it ordered six with options on a further six. All told, it operated 14 One-Elevens, the first of which was delivered in March 1965 and went into service the following month. Braniff was one of three US airlines to order the One-Eleven, the others being American Airlines, which ordered 30, and regional carrier Mohawk, 14. The One-Eleven was among Britain's most successful post-war jet airliner programmes, having been launched by an order for ten placed by Britain's biggest, and newest, independent airline, British United Airways (BUA) in 1961, from the newly created British Aircraft Corporation. (BAE SYSTEMS Heritage)

Published by Key Books
An imprint of Key Publishing Ltd
PO Box 100
Stamford
Lincs PE19 1XQ

www.keypublishing.com

Original edition published as *Aeroplane Classic Airliner: The BAC One-Eleven* © 2013, edited by Bruce Hales-Dutton

Unless otherwise credited, all photos are © Key Archive

This edition © 2022

ISBN 978 1 80282 367 7

Typeset by SJmagic DESIGN SERVICES, India.

Contents

Introduction

It was half a century ago, on 20 August 1963, that the British Aircraft Corporation (BAC) One-Eleven, Britain's latest jet airliner, flew for the first time. Its 26-minute maiden flight was brief but successful. BAC, which designed the airframe, Rolls-Royce, manufacturer of the Spey engines that powered it, and British United Airways (BUA) whose order for ten One-Elevens had launched the new airliner, breathed a collective sigh of relief: so far so good.

There was indeed a lot riding on the One-Eleven. For BAC, which had resulted from the consolidation of the nation's aircraft industry from 27 companies to just three major airframe builders, the new jet promised salvation. BUA was also a young company having, like BAC, been formed in 1960. Its experience of ordering new airliners, let alone jets, was strictly limited. Usually, it was one of the state-owned operators, the British Overseas Airways Corporation (BOAC) or British European Airways (BEA), which formulated the specification of any new civil aircraft. But the One-Eleven was the first major airliner to be launched by an order from an independent airline. The outline of its specification was hammered out by Sir George Edwards, BAC's managing director, and Freddie (later Sir Freddie) Laker, managing director of BUA. Perhaps that is why the One-Eleven was able to appeal to such a wide variety of airlines, including American ones. In fact, it was the first British jet to be ordered off the drawing board by a US airline. The result was that the One-Eleven was one of Britain's biggest dollar earners.

Even though BEA initially showed no interest in the new airliner, the twin-jet was flying in its colours before the decade was out. Inevitably, the state-owned carrier wanted to specify features of its own. Soon, the One-Eleven was operating around the world, and in Britain it formed the backbone of the short-haul fleet. During the 1970s and early '80s, it was the staple of the inclusive tour holiday business operated by airlines like Dan-Air, Laker Airways, British Caledonian Airways (BCal), Monarch Airlines, Autair/Court Line and British Island Airways.

At the time of the One-Eleven's first flight, BAC seemed to have stolen a march on its American rivals. It was comfortably ahead of the similarly configured DC-9, and the Boeing 737 was barely a gleam in Boeing's eye at the time. So why was it that Douglas went on to sell over 1,000 DC-9s (to say nothing of the developed MD-80 and Boeing 717) while BAC shifted only 244 One-Elevens? The answer to that question is just one part of the fascinating tale of the One-Eleven. What follows is the full story of its concept and design against the troubled background of the industry's consolidation and of its entry into service. The One-Eleven was undoubtedly a great British achievement; however, its success was conditional and anybody studying the aircraft's history is left with the feeling that it represents an opportunity lost.

Chapter 1

Downsizing an Industry

I t was described as one of the most important documents ever laid before parliament, and the new defence policy contained in a White Paper published by the government of Prime Minister Harold Macmillan in April 1957 was certainly controversial.

The cornerstone was the ending of conscription and, with it, National Service. The intention was to redress a situation in which defence spending had reached 7 per cent of gross national product. In the Western world, only the Unites States was spending more on defence than Britain.

The White Paper also contained the alarming admission that the only effective defence against nuclear attack was a credible ability to retaliate in kind. But the paragraphs for which it is now best remembered are those that foreshadowed a major change in aircraft procurement for the Royal Air Force (RAF). The policy, of which Defence Minister Duncan Sandys was identified as the chief architect, heralded the end of manned combat aircraft. But there were exceptions. The P.1 supersonic fighter, later known as the Lightning, was too far advanced to cancel, and there would be a replacement for the Canberra bomber.

Several other advanced military aircraft projects were summarily cancelled, and it was clear that the result of Sandys' policy would be a drastic reduction in the size of the British aircraft industry. At the end of World War Two, there were 27 airframe manufacturers and eight aero-engine builders. Although a reduction in these numbers seemed inevitable, the outbreak of the Korean War and the deepening of East–West tensions postponed the industry's rationalisation. There were mergers, but by the end of the decade, there were still 25 airframe and seven engine builders.

Two products of BAC and both operated by BUA: it could only be Gatwick during the 1960s. BAC One-Eleven G-ASJG shares the apron with a VC10. A Series 200 aircraft, 'JG was delivered to BUA in July 1965.

The supersonic English Electric P.1 was the only manned fighter project intended for RAF service to escape cancellation under Duncan Sandys' 1957 defence policy. The prototype, WG760, which flew for the first time in August 1954, is pictured here. Six years later, the first production examples, now known as the Lightning and featuring such visual differences as a revised cockpit canopy, dorsal spine and the characteristic pointed intake-mounted radome, entered RAF service.

Amalgamate or die

The government had made it clear in September 1957 that a contract for the Canberra replacement, known as 239, could only be placed with a group of firms. In future, there would be work on major aircraft projects for three, or at most four, groups. This was widely interpreted as the government putting a pistol to the industry's head. The watchword was clearly amalgamate or die, but then Britain still had more airframe companies than the US.

It was confidently expected that a reduction in UK military orders would be made up by sales of new civil types, such as the Vickers Vanguard and Bristol Britannia then under development, as well as other new aircraft planned for the state-owned airlines, BEA and BOAC. But with the UK armed services accounting for 70 per cent of the industry's business, it was clear that Sandys' defence policy would bring a major contraction in the UK aircraft industry.

Intensive negotiations

Indeed, in little less than four years, the industry was consolidated into three airframe and two engine companies. The most intensive negotiations took place during the last nine months. And there was one minister in particular at the heart of the process: Duncan Sandys. After the 1959 General Election, Macmillan put him in charge of an expanded aviation ministry. Sandys now had responsibility for both military and civil matters. Clearly, he was the minister in charge of aircraft industry consolidation.

The rationalisation process was sweetened by promises that government support for research and development would continue and that repayable launch aid for promising civil aircraft and engines would be introduced. It meant the passing of some of British aviation's great names, but it laid the foundations for a stronger domestic aircraft industry.

Two projects in particular were the catalysts for merger: TSR. 2, formerly OR 339, and a new medium-haul airliner for BEA, which was later to become the Hawker Siddeley Trident. The convoluted process of bidding for Trident eventually saw the de Havilland Aircraft Company join the Hawker Siddeley Group in one of the two major new blocs.

Initially, it had seemed as if English Electric, fresh from its success with the Canberra and the supersonic P.1, would lead TSR. 2 development on the basis of its P.17 proposal. But the company reckoned without the influence of Sir George Edwards, managing director of Vickers' aircraft division. He got wind of the government's preference for English Electric and during the summer of 1958 lobbied hard to secure leadership for Vickers.

The Air Staff in particular supported Edwards and Vickers. In any case, it was clear that, unlike English Electric, Vickers was short of military work. Its turboprop Vanguard was not enjoying the sales success of the Viscount, which had been designed by Edwards. So, by early 1959, it was clear that Vickers would be leading a 50-50 collaboration on the TSR. 2 with English Electric.

But while the two companies were considering the options for a merger of their aviation interests, de Havilland had entered the picture with its DH 121 airliner project. There were talks between the three companies' leaders that could have resulted in a Vickers–English Electric–de Havilland merger. Had this gone ahead, it would have resulted in a powerful grouping that, some historians suggest, might have been a major force competing in world markets during the 1960s and '70s.

The TSR. 2, designed to meet operational requirement OR 339, played a significant role in the consolidation of the British aircraft industry in the early 1960s, after the government made it clear that bids for the project should only come from merged groups of manufacturers, rather than individual companies. Having played its crucial role, BAC's TSR.2 was controversially cancelled by the incoming Labour government. Pictured here is XR220, which was retained for Olympus engine development is towed into the Cosford hangar early in 1973.

Above and below: The VC11 was Vickers' attempt to produce a short- to medium-haul airliner, but it soon become clear that the airlines were not attracted by the economics offered by four-engines where three or even two would do. These models produced by Vickers clearly show that the VC11 was very much a truncated down VC10. (BAE SYSTEMS Heritage)

The stumbling block, however, was that, in addition to the four-jet VC10 and the enhanced Super VC10, Vickers was hoping to launch a new medium-haul airliner. It was larger than the DH 121 but would be aimed at similar markets. It was essentially a scaled-down VC10 and known as the VC11.

It was at this point that Sandys intervened. Now established in his new job, he was fretting that things were not moving fast enough. With his political clout, he was able to unravel some of the tensions within Whitehall and bring greater influence to bear with both the Treasury and industry chiefs.

In private, Sandys talked about his 'marriage bureau'. In practice, he was able to use his position to raise the tempo of the rationalisation process. In a series of meetings with industry chiefs, he not only offered promises of continued government support for research and development but also hammered out a system of repayable launch aid.

Sandys told Vickers and de Havilland that they would have to resolve their differences over the DH 121 and the VC11. He therefore welcomed the news that English Electric and Vickers were considering a hostile take-over bid for de Havilland. But this idea foundered because Vickers and English Electric still had to decide the precise mechanics of their own partnership.

A further complicating factor was Vickers' financial position. By late 1959, the company's losses on the Vanguard were put at £147m. Further losses were expected with the VC10. Moreover, development costs for the VC11 were estimated at £88m. It was clear to Sandys that Vickers was approaching a crisis that could force it out of the civil aircraft business. On 17 December 1959, he presented to the cabinet a plan to secure the industry's future. At its heart was the support for research and development, as well as his idea for repayable launch aid for civil projects to be recovered by a levy on sales. Sandys suggested the government would pay half the VC11's launch costs.

The Trident was another catalyst for aircraft industry consolidation as various company groupings attempted to meet a British European Airways (BEA) requirement for a short- to medium-haul jet. The airline originally selected the de Havilland DH 121, powered by three Rolls-Royce Medway engines, but a downturn in traffic prompted the airline to insist on a smaller aircraft. The result was the Hawker Siddeley Trident in which the Rolls-Royce Spey was specified in place of the promising Medway, which was subsequently abandoned. It was the Spey's availability that also influenced the design of the One-Eleven. Here, a Trident Two, the variant most pilots preferred, shows off its sleek lines.

The Vanguard was Vickers' first attempt at producing a Viscount successor. Launch customer BEA wanted a bigger aircraft with enhanced levels of passenger comfort, and this the Rolls-Royce Tyne-powered Vanguard delivered. But the trouble was it was another turboprop at a time when jets were becoming available for use on short-haul routes. As a result, just 44 Vanguards were produced.

The Vickers VC1 Viking was derived from the wartime Wellington bomber and was Britain's first post-war airliner. It was also George Edwards' first project following his appointment as the company's chief designer. He later described the Viking as a British version of the Douglas DC-3, although far fewer (161) were produced. The Viking was to be the backbone of BEA's fleet in the 1950s, and here the airline's *Verdant* receives attention at Rome's Ciampino airport as a Viscount approaches to land.

As the world's first turbine-powered airliner, the Viscount holds a special place in aviation history. Its use by BEA transformed the airline's fortunes by bringing new standards of passenger comfort to make it Europe's favourite airliner. Its success also meant substantial export sales and when Capital Airlines pioneered turbine power in the US, the total value of its order for 60 Viscounts made it Britain's biggest single post-war dollar export order until then. It was well and truly put in the shade by the Viscount's successor when American Airlines ordered 30 One-Elevens.

BAC emerges

The way was clear for the formation of the new group. The British Aircraft Corporation would involve 40 per cent shareholdings by Vickers and English Electric, with 20 per cent held by the Bristol Aeroplane Company. The final piece of the jigsaw was slotted into place in 1960 when BAC acquired 70 per cent of Hunting Aircraft. This was to be a crucial move in ensuring the new group's survival. It would also lead to the development of one of Britain's best-known post-war civil aircraft.

The new group was certainly not overburdened with work. In addition to the TSR.2 (later cancelled) and the VC10 – the prospects of which were stunted by the parochial BOAC requirements to which it had been designed – there was the Anglo-French supersonic airliner project in which Bristol had been heavily involved, but little else – apart, that is, from two short- to medium-haul airliner projects.

The Hunting H.107 and the VC11 were very different concepts, yet they were to be brought together to provide the basis for a new short-haul airliner that would bring much-needed relief for the hard-pressed new group.

The four-engined VC10 was designed to meet challenging requirements issued by British Overseas Airways Corporation (BOAC) for an aircraft capable of operating from short runways on its African route network. As it happened, BOAC later decided it preferred the rival Boeing 707 at a time when Vickers was forced to admit it had underestimated the cost of developing the VC10. Production of the VC10, however, was supported by aviation minister Duncan Sandys as it fitted well with his plans for industry consolidation. Nevertheless, the VC10 was popular with passengers and served BOAC, and later British Airways, well. This stylish BOAC postcard emphasises the aircraft's sleek lines.

The Vickers V.1000 was an advanced jet transport that could have offered trans-Atlantic travel but whose cancellation in 1955 just six months before the first prototype's projected maiden flight was considered such a mistake by Sir George Edwards. Years later, he was to describe its demise as 'the biggest blunder of all'.

SIR GEORGE EDWARDS

If any one man can be identified as the father of the BAC One-Eleven, it must surely be George Robert Freeman Edwards. And that is particularly appropriate because, in 1948, he designed its predecessor, the turbo-prop Vickers Viscount.

At that time, Edwards was Vickers' chief designer, having joined the company at Weybridge, Surrey, in 1935. Before that, he had been working as a junior structural engineer at London's docks. He was interviewed for a job in Vickers's drawing office, which he was offered at a weekly salary of £5.25, 25p more than he was expecting.

Edwards was born 27 years earlier above his father's toyshop near Chingford, Essex. His mother died two weeks after his birth and he was brought up by an aunt. He won a scholarship to South West Essex Technical College at Walthamstow, where he showed a talent for mathematics. Moving on to the West Ham Municipal College, he learned to be a practical engineer, then took a BSc in Engineering from London University.

When war broke out in 1939, Edwards became experimental works manager. One of his first tasks was to design an aerial minesweeping system for Coastal Command Wellingtons. Edwards

Part of the reason for the One-Eleven's success in the US market was the personal chemistry that developed between Sir George Edwards and Braniff International Airways president Charles 'Chuck' Beard. As Edwards noted: 'If he and I hadn't got on all right there would have been no business'. The Texas-based airline became the first US airline to operate the One-Eleven, having ordered the type off the drawing board. Here, Beard (left) and Edwards (in trademark hat) are pictured with a BUA One-Eleven at Hurn. (BAE SYSTEMS Heritage)

had been working with Vickers' chief designer Rex Pierson, whom he succeeded in 1945. In his new post, Edwards was responsible for the Viking airliner, together with its military variants the Valetta and the Varsity. Then came the jet-powered Valiant, the first of the RAF's three nuclear deterrent V-bomber types.

When it appeared in 1948, the Viscount was not only the world's first turboprop airliner to operate passenger services, it was also the first British airliner to make significant headway in the American domestic airline market. A total of 445 aircraft were sold to 38 airlines, including BEA.

As managing director of Vickers-Armstrongs (Aircraft) from 1953, Edwards remained responsible for overall technical direction of the Viscount's successor, the Vanguard. But this large, four-engined turboprop was being marketed just as jets were superseding propeller-driven types.

Even before that, however, Vickers was on the brink of pulling off a major success with the V.1000 military transport jet and its civilian counterpart the VC7. Edwards described the project's cancellation in 1955 as 'the biggest blunder of all'. He was convinced it could have upstaged both the DC-8 and Boeing 707, which were not to enter service until the end of the decade. Some compensation was his knighthood in 1957.

The VC10, with its four rear-mounted engines, was designed in response to a challenging specification issued by BOAC, which wanted an aircraft that could operate from short, hot and high airports in Africa and Asia. The aircraft proved popular with passengers, but its operating economics were inferior to the 707 and only a relative handful were built.

Edwards played a key part in the creation of BAC. In 1961, he was appointed managing director of its operating arm and, in 1968, chairman of the company itself. In that role, he guided the design and development of the One-Eleven short-haul airliner.

Without Edwards' patience and perseverance when dealing with politicians and his counterparts across the Channel, it is doubtful if the supersonic Concorde project would have come to fruition, let alone survived. Edwards appointment to the Order of Merit in 1971 not only acknowledged his overall contribution to British aviation but also his participation in the development of Concorde.

Edwards retired in 1975, after 40 years devoted to the British aircraft industry. During that time, he was recognised not just as a talented engineer but also as a consummate salesman and businessman whose organisational skills helped ensure that the industry continued to punch above its weight in world markets. Down-to-earth and lacking in pomposity, Edwards was also known for his pithy comments. He died in 2003 aged 94.

Chapter 2

New Manufacturer, New Airline, New Design

I n the first half of 1961, the future of the newly formed British Aircraft Corporation was still in the balance. Both the TSR.2 and the Anglo-French supersonic airliner project were coming under increasing and hostile scrutiny. At the same time, the future of the four-jet VC10 airliner was in doubt and the turboprop Vanguard was not achieving the hoped-for sales success.

This was the situation in May 1961 when the BAC board agreed to launch a new short-haul airliner. The appearance of the BAC One-Eleven has been described as little short of miraculous. But it was to be the last airliner built by BAC and the last but one to be produced in Britain, the final complete aircraft being the BAe 146. It was also to be Sir George Edwards' last aircraft to enter service.

A year earlier, BAC had agreed to buy the aircraft interests of the Hunting Group. The most obvious result was the acquisition of the successful Jet Provost family of jet trainers, but it also brought an interesting airliner project. In 1955, Hunting had initiated a design study into a short-haul airliner with seating for 30 passengers in a four-abreast layout. It was to be powered by a pair of Bristol Orpheus engines and featured modestly swept wings and tail surfaces. The project was known as the P.107. Hunting was so confident, it even had the registration G-APOH allocated to the first prototype.

Above left: En route to the future. The Hunting H.107 progressed little further than this fuselage section, pictured here on the back of a transporter lorry in this atmospheric Hunting Percival picture dated 17 February 1956. It was to perform a vital role as the basis for the BAC One-Eleven.

Above right: It was in 1955 that Hunting began design studies into a 30-seat short-haul transport with rear-mounted Bristol Orpheus engines and modestly swept-back wings. Hunting was so confident about the soundness of its ideas that it reserved the registration G-APOH in July 1958, although this overhead shot depicts a more speculative registration. After the company's acquisition in 1960 by the newly formed BAC, the H.107 inspired the BAC One-Eleven, although by that time it had become bigger and featured a pair of Rolls-Royce Speys in place of the original Orpheus units. The One-Eleven also adopted a 'T' tail in place of the H.107's cruciform layout.

Scaled-down VC10

It was not, though, to be built. Vickers had been approaching the concept of a medium- to short-haul airliner from the opposite end of the spectrum. The VC11 had been intended to meet a BEA requirement for an 80-seater with a 1,000-mile range. The airline had seen it as a three-engined aircraft, while Vickers was thinking in terms of what was essentially a scaled down VC10. It was to be powered by four Rolls-Royce RB.163 engines.

Edwards believed the aircraft should have a wider appeal and was convinced the VC11 could have achieved success. But BEA thought it was too big, and Edwards was reluctant to reduce its appeal into world markets by making it smaller. Vickers withdrew from the BEA contest but continued work on the project.

BEA, meanwhile, selected the de Havilland DH 121 powered by a trio of Rolls-Royce RB.141 Medway by-pass engines. Historians would later remark on the similarity between the DH 121 as originally proposed and the highly successful Boeing 727 that was to become the best-selling airliner of its era. But a fall in passenger numbers made BEA uneasy about the project, and it decided the DH 121 was too big. Not only was the aircraft's appeal reduced, but the promising Medway engine was abandoned.

To Edwards this was a major blow, a blunder ranking with the cancellation of the V.1000. He believed that, had the Medway been chosen for the TSR.2, it might not have been cancelled in 1965. Of greater

Even in its early form, the H.107 looked a more likely bet than the VC11, a model of which is pictured here.
(BAE SYSTEMS Heritage)

Another view of H.107, showing the rear-mounted engines and mildly swept-back wings.

significance to the One-Eleven, the Medway's cancellation deprived it of an engine that might have powered developed versions and prolonged the programme.

That, though, was in the future in 1959, when Vickers was offering the VC11 to the airlines. Trans-Canada Air Lines and Continental Airlines both showed an interest in the project. At that stage, Continental was convinced that it represented the best medium-haul jet for its route network. At the same time, the British government, which was then trying to persuade Vickers to merge with English Electric, offered to fund 50 per cent of the VC11's launch costs, subject to the project going ahead.

This was looking less certain, however. Market resistance to the idea of a short- to medium-haul jet airliner with four engines was growing at a time when Sud Aviation in France was offering the twin-jet Caravelle with its two rear-mounted engines. As it turned out, this was to be a trend-setting configuration. Edwards conceded that a four-engined aircraft would have higher operating costs. But even more daunting was the 72 sales the new aircraft would have to achieve to qualify for government launching aid. Edwards was becoming doubtful that that could be achieved.

Joint project

No wonder the Vickers engineers became interested in the H.107. At the time of BAC's formation, they appraised the design and pronounced it sound. In May 1960, Edwards and Arthur Summers, Hunting's managing director, agreed to take it forward as a joint project. The renamed BAC107 featured five-abreast seating for up to 56 passengers and two Bristol BS75 engines offering about 7,000lb of thrust each. A cruising speed of 500mph and range of 600 miles were expected. Like the Caravelle, and, for that matter, the H.107, the engines were to be mounted on either side of the rear fuselage. The BAC107 also had a T-tail with the horizontal surfaces mounted at the top of the fin and rudder.

Studies conducted in 1960 suggested a market for the aircraft of around 600 aircraft. Significantly, it was expected 80 could be sold in the US. The key attributes were now the ability to offer increased frequency at low cost on existing jet routes, to offer better operating economics than bigger jets on shorter routes and to introduce jets to less developed markets like South America.

BAC sales staff had talked to over 80 airlines around the world and brought back expressions of interest from the majority. More significantly, the feedback suggested that the aircraft's weight would rise and there were doubts about the Bristol engines' ability to handle it. Among the interested airlines was the recently formed BUA. It was looking for a jet Viscount 800 replacement capable of reaching Malta from Gatwick. At the time, the airline was conducting lucrative trooping operations for the Ministry of Defence, as well as inclusive tour holiday operations to Mediterranean holiday resorts. By contrast, US airlines like Texas-based Braniff International were seeking a jet to fly very short sectors with rapid turn arounds. More differences arose when it became clear that BUA wanted more fuel capacity while Braniff was not interested in the projected ventral stairs.

A decision now had to be taken on the VC11's future. Edwards had visited North America earlier in the year to settle matters between it and the BAC107, and it was clear to him that opinion was now favouring the twin-jet. US airlines' reservations about the rear-engined layout were changing following United Airlines' operating experience with the Caravelle. But it also seemed that the BAC107 was a little too small.

On his return, Edwards reported to the BAC board that at least 13 more rows of seats would be needed and that there was a demand for more on-board equipment. This would push up the weight.

The early trend-setter among short-haul jets was the Sud Caravelle. News of its development prompted BEA to revise its belief that it would be relying on turboprops well into the 1960s. When they entered service, Air France's new Caravelles lopped 20 minutes off the journey time from Paris to Heathrow and 50 minutes from Nice. The French jet also featured the rear-mounted engines adopted by the BAC One-Eleven and which Hunting had specified for its projected H.107.

Production of the One-Eleven is well under way at Hurn in this early '60s shot of half a dozen examples on the production line headed by one for BUA. It was BUA's order for ten that enabled the BAC board to agree to the twin-jet's launch.

As a result, he noted, 'the required payload/range configuration was outside the capacity of the original project'. In March 1961, a decision was therefore taken for the new airliner to use Spey engines, a powerplant already selected for BEA's Trident, which was set to make its maiden flight in a year's time. Edwards was confident that the revised aircraft would be bought by major US domestic airlines.

VC11 cancelled

It was also clear that the VC11 was a dead duck. The BAC board agreed to cancel it and to approach the government for launch aid: the requirement was for half the development costs and half the production commitments. Aviation minister Peter Thorneycroft agreed to transfer the £9.75m originally scheduled for the VC11.

The new airliner was taking shape. It now had government funding and it had a new name: henceforth, it would be known as the BAC One-Eleven. It also had a launch customer. As it happened, BUA was striving to become established as Britain's biggest independent airline at a time when BAC was trying to find customers for its newest project.

The airline's managing director was the ebullient Freddie Laker, a man whose name probably justifies the prefix 'legendary'. Indeed, in later life, Laker took a delight in weaving the legends of his achievements and particularly the way he agreed to become launch customer for the One-Eleven. According to Laker's biographers, he and Edwards discussed the matter over a dinner arranged by BAC

Three Laker Airways stewardesses pose for the camera with their employer's first BAC One-Eleven under construction at Hurn (left). G-AVBW (right) was delivered in February 1967. Freddie Laker had quit as managing director of BUA and decided to start his own airline. It might have seemed logical for the man who had chosen the One-Eleven back in 1961 to repeat the process when running his own airline, but the astute Laker had already carefully considered his options, including the competing Douglas DC-9 and the Boeing 737. (BAE SYSTEMS Heritage)

marketing director Geoffrey Knight. For most of the meal, Edwards and Laker thrashed out the key features of a deal that also included more performance for the aircraft than BAC was offering.

With the coffee came agreement. Laker told Edwards: 'I'll take ten if it'll do what you say it will'.

It was a key moment in the history of the One-Eleven. It also led to the BAC board's decision to launch the aircraft. It was not, however, an easy decision. A lot was riding on it: the future of one of Britain's two major airframe builders and also that of the nation's biggest independent airline. 'In fact,' Edwards said years later, 'it worked out all right'.

Once the decision had been taken to buy the aircraft, the scene was now set for a period of hard-bargaining between manufacturer and customer over the One-Eleven's performance and price. Laker delegated the job to his executive assistant Mick Sidebotham, who found himself dealing with BAC's airline development engineer John Prothero Thomas. Sidebotham had been instructed to ensure that any additional features did not increase the aircraft's weight and reduce its payload. At times, Laker became directly involved in the negotiations. It was an experience that Prothero Thomas found to be a bruising one.

Yet Laker's insistence on the aircraft's ability to carry a full load of passengers the 1,000 miles between Gatwick–Malta, non-stop, with a 14,000lb payload, meant a more versatile and more saleable aircraft. The improved payload/range characteristics insisted upon by Laker increased its appeal in overseas markets, particularly the US. But surprisingly, given the intensity of these negotiations, the actual price BUA would pay for the aircraft was decided rather less formally at, of all places, the paddock at Sandown Park racecourse. There, Knight and Laker agreed BUA would get its One-Elevens for £740,000 per aircraft. It was a bargain.

BUA's order

On 9 May 1961, BAC and BUA announced that the One-Eleven was being launched on the back of BUA's order for ten aircraft worth a total of £8m. In addition, the airline had options for five more aircraft. The One-Eleven had become the first major airliner not to be launched with an order from one of the state-owned airlines. That meant that it would appeal to a wider market rather than being tailored to the requirements of BOAC or BEA. Perhaps that is why it comfortably outsold the Trident (117 customer deliveries) and the VC10 (54).

The May 1961 announcement also indicated that the first flight was planned for the second quarter of 1963, with certification by mid-1964 and first deliveries to BUA that autumn. It was a challenging timetable.

Right: A happy group of passengers on board the first BAC One-Eleven service flown by Laker Airways. The man himself has broken off from a conversation to smile for the camera. Freddie Laker was one of the key figures behind the original launch of the One-Eleven when he was managing director of BUA. (BAE SYSTEMS Heritage)

Below: Bournemouth's Hurn Airport, 20 August 1963: the prototype One-Eleven pictured before its first flight. There was heavy rain that day, as indicated by the wet apron.

FREDDIE LAKER

If Sir George Edwards was the father of the BAC One-Eleven then perhaps Freddie Laker can be identified as its godfather. As managing director of BUA, it was his order for ten aircraft that enabled the new twin-jet to be launched.

The negotiations, which led to the announcement of the order in May 1961, were characterised by an uncompromising negotiating style that Laker had learnt over the preceding two decades.

He was born in Kent in modest circumstances but later claimed to have inherited his entrepreneurial skills from his mother, Hannah, and he would name his airline's first DC-10, *Canterbury Belle,* after her.

It was in that city that he also claimed to have seen the sight that prompted his choice of career when he watched the German airship *Hindenburg* and an Imperial Airways airliner fly over the cathedral. He started literally on the ground floor on his 16th birthday in 1938. His first job was sweeping floors at the Short Brothers' Rochester factory. During the war, he served with the Air Transport Auxiliary, ending up with piloting and engineering qualifications.

After the war, Laker went into business for himself and borrowed the money to buy 12 Handley Page Halifaxes. He did a deal with a company called Bond Air Services to operate the aircraft on the Berlin Airlift. It was to make him a wealthy man.

His company, Southend-based Aviation Traders, initially bought and sold aircraft parts but moved into aircraft design with the Rolls-Royce Dart-powered Accountant airliner. It flopped, but the later Carvair, a DC-4 converted to carry cars, was a success and was operated by Channel Air Bridge, launched as an offshoot of Laker's Air Charter operation.

He sold Air Charter to Airwork but returned to the fold as managing director of BUA, which had been created through the merger of Airwork and the aviation interests of Hunting-Clan. In 1965, though, Laker fell out with BUA's chairman and left to form his own Laker Airways, primarily to serve the inclusive tour holiday market.

It was then that he conceived the idea of low-cost scheduled trans-Atlantic air services, and although the UK and US governments initially resisted, Laker, with his expansive manner and flair for publicity, eventually prevailed. The first Skytrain left Gatwick for New York in September 1977.

Although primarily aimed at people on low incomes, it became popular with business travellers despite the lack of frills. By 1981, over two million passengers had travelled on Skytrain, which had expanded to serve San Francisco, Miami, Los Angeles and Tampa. But the established carriers responded by slashing fares. That, combined with economic recession, forced Laker Airways into bankruptcy in 1982. He had also conceived plans to operate 140 European routes to open up the market to lower fares. After Skytrain, Laker left the UK to form Laker Airways (Bahamas) with two Boeing 727s flying gamblers from the US to Grand Bahama. He died in Miami in 2006.

Chapter 3

Anatomy of the Bus-Stop Jet

Not surprisingly, Sir George Edwards was given overall responsibility for the One-Eleven. BAC's production director, A W E Houghton, reported to him, while Arthur Summers, former Hunting managing director, was in charge of production and development. B Stephenson, who had been Vickers' engineering director, was given technical responsibility for the design.

With key figures from the three companies now involved, it was decided to divide production between their main facilities. Hurn (Vickers) would therefore design and construct the front and centre fuselage, Filton (Bristol) would be responsible for the rear fuselage and tail, Luton (Hunting) the wings, flaps and ailerons and Weybridge (Vickers) the nose and main undercarriage legs, wing skins and wing centre sections. The main assembly line would be at Hurn, although a few aircraft were to be built at Weybridge.

From the start, it was clear that as a short-haul aircraft the One-Eleven would represent a compromise between high speed and cost. The avoidance of complex high-lift devices dictated the choice of wings with a 20-dgeree sweep-back. This would permit a cruising Mach number of 0.78 at 25,000ft or 550mph. Because of its role as a 'bus-stop jet', the aircraft needed a robust and fatigue-resistant structure to withstand a life of quick turnarounds, take-offs and landings.

Early days: BAC One-Eleven fuselage jigs are shown here under construction at Hurn in this picture taken in April 1962. (BAE SYSTEMS Heritage)

Self-sufficient

To prevent delays caused by lack of ground equipment at small airports, the One-Eleven was intended to be largely self-sufficient, with its own auxiliary power unit and airstairs. The freight bay would be positioned at waist-height, with servicing and fuelling points conveniently located. Indeed, refuelling was intended to be a ten-minute operation.

Even before the aircraft's first flight, it was decided there would be three main variants: the baseline Series 200 and the Series 300 and 400 with more powerful Spey 25 engines and airframes cleared for operation at heavier weights. The Series 300s and 400s were intended for sectors of up to 1,500 miles and consequently featured a beefed-up wing structure and centre fuel tank. The additional weight required a stronger undercarriage, bigger brakes and lift-dumpers. The Series 400 was essentially the Series 300 equipped for the US market.

The One-Eleven's primary structure was designed to the failsafe principle with alternative load paths provided so that failure or partial failure of a main structural member would not cause the collapse of the main structure or weaken it beyond limits. Where it was not possible to provide a multi-path structure, the stress level was intended to be so low that it would be protected from catastrophic failure resulting from cracks. It was this philosophy, allied to the attention paid to corrosion-resistance, which

Taking shape: One-Eleven fuselages under construction at Hurn. Note the fascinating detail visible in this shot, including the safety notices suspended from the ceiling. (BAE SYSTEMS Heritage)

Bare bones: inside a One-Eleven fuselage under construction at Hurn. (BAE SYSTEMS Heritage)

no doubt contributed to the reputation for robustness the One-Eleven would win during its service life. According to one experienced captain, the aircraft was 'built like a tank'.

The structure was mostly a conventional built-up type with light-alloy machined sections used in some fuselage frames, the wing torque-boxes and door and flight-deck window surrounds. The basic fuselage featured rolled skin plating with a minimum thickness of 0.048in in the pressurised area. It was built in three sections: front, centre and rear, with the centre incorporating the torque boxes for wing attachment. The rear fuselage, incorporating the engine mountings and fin frames, was designed as a single structure in unit with the vertical fin.

Of conventional torque box design, the wings incorporated three spars with integrally machined stringers on the upper and lower skinning. The ribs gave the wing its basic shape as well as torsional rigidity, and the wings incorporated integral fuel tanks. The rear spar provided mounting points for the ailerons and flaps as well as the undercarriage mountings. The ailerons featured four hinges to provide a degree of redundancy.

At the rear of the fuselage, the engines were suspended from a pair of steel beams. Trunnions attached to the engines were mounted on the front beam transmitting thrust loads to the main structure via tubular struts to the rear pressure bulkhead and a machined light alloy beam located between the two engine frames.

The wing torsion boxes doubled as integral fuel tanks and offered capacity of 2,200 imperial gallons. On all variants apart from the baseline Series 200, there was an 850-gallon tank contained in the centre-section box. Additional fuel capacity could be provided at the rear of the forward freight hold.

Duplicated systems

The aircraft's systems were designed on the basis of duplication to provide protection in the event of failure. Two generators were driven from the engines with a third operated by the APU providing ground power, although there was provision for use of an external supply. Similarly, the hydraulics comprised two independent systems each with their own reservoirs, pumps and piping. Each system was to be powered by a different engine and independently powered the control surfaces and the flight-deck windscreen wipers. Similarly, there were duplicated air conditioning, de-icing and emergency oxygen systems.

The landing gear, which was designed to free-fall in the event of a complete hydraulic system failure, incorporated a twin-wheel nose gear and a pair of single-axle two-wheel main units. The hydraulic braking system incorporated dual redundancy and an anti-skid system. Hydraulic actuators provided steering power via a flight deck hand wheel.

The One-Eleven was designed for two-crew operation. This made it the first jet airliner in the world to be so configured, although there was an additional seat behind the pilots and fittings for a fourth. Great attention was paid to cockpit visibility with six large windows and slim pillars. Basic instruments were arranged in a 'T' ahead of each pilot and incorporated the Collins FD-108 Flight Director System. Subsidiary controls were mounted in the roof panels, and these were generally pre-set before flight to avoid continual in-flight monitoring. A central pedestal incorporated engine throttles and controls as well as controls for speed brakes, flaps and trimmers.

This view of a BUA BAC One-Eleven in the final stages of assembly at Hurn clearly shows the wing flaps in their extended position. (BAE SYSTEMS Heritage)

Another view of the One-Eleven production line at Hurn, headed by one to which British United titles have been applied. (BAE SYSTEMS Heritage)

The cabin layout was designed to offer maximum flexibility so that seating configurations and cabin layouts could be altered to suit particular types of operation. The baseline aircraft offered four-abreast seating for 16 first-class passengers plus 49 tourist class five-abreast. A moveable bulkhead divided the classes. The design enabled seat pitch to be reduced to 29in, but a typical all-tourist arrangement provided 74 seats with 34in pitch. The later Series 500s could accommodate up to 119 passengers. Cabins were initially fitted with luggage racks, but in 1977 a 'wide-body look' was introduced with lidded lockers for new-build aircraft and offered as a retro-fit on existing aircraft.

Two galley units were provided on the right side of the aircraft forward and aft of the galley service door. There were also two toilets, one forward and on the left and the other aft and to the right. There were two passenger doors, one forward of the passenger cabin on the left-hand side, while the other was a ventral door in the rear pressure bulkhead. Although both doors were offered with integral airstairs, Braniff ordered its aircraft without the ventral units while BUA and BEA dispensed with the forward airstairs on their Series 201s and 510s, respectively.

Above: This rear view looking forwards shows a One-Eleven nacelle awaiting its Spey engine and also some of the detail of its attachment to the fuselage. (BAE SYSTEMS Heritage)

Left: One-Eleven production reaches a new stage as the nose section of the first production Series 475 takes shape at Hurn. The variant was intended for use in remote areas not previously served by jets, which is why its builders publicised it as 'the big jet for the small fields.' The prototype first flew in August 1970, and Compania de Aviation Faucett of Peru received its first example the following July.

In a special supplement on the One-Eleven published in February 1965, *The Aeroplane* noted that in fulfilling the needs of both the aircraft's operating environment and the demands of its customers and their passengers, 'BAC has mounted a programme the like of which has never before been seen anywhere in the world for this class of aeroplane'.

This had been demonstrated by two factors. The first, the journal said, 'has been the provision of high quality and short lead time production facilities. The second has been fulfilling the demands of engineering integrity necessary in every aspect of the aircraft itself and its supporting functions because of the short flight duty cycle with frequent take-offs and landings'.

One-Elevens under construction at Hurn in 1971. Both aircraft in the foreground are Series 475s. The one nearest the camera was delivered to Air Pacific of Fiji and the aircraft next to it started operations with Air Malawi on its central and southern African routes in March 1972.

Left: The first production One-Eleven Series 475 is pictured here being moved forwards on the Hurn production line on its own wheels in February 1971. The aircraft had been ordered by Faucett of Peru and was scheduled to be delivered in July in time for the country's 150th anniversary celebrations.

Below: BUA's second One-Eleven, registered G-ASJB, nears completion on the Hurn production line. The aircraft first flew in February 1964 but was badly damaged in a crash at Wisley a month later. Plans to rebuild the aircraft were later abandoned. Note the row of Spey engines in the foreground in this atmospheric colour shot.

POWER FOR THE ONE-ELEVEN

The BAC One-Eleven was essentially designed around a pair of Rolls-Royce Spey turbo fan engines.

The Spey's heritage can be traced back to 1958, when Rolls-Royce decided to start work on a new engine specifically for airliner use. The unit was based on the Conway turbofan, which powered the VC10, but having a higher by-pass ratio.

Given the project number RB.141 and later called the Medway, the 12,000lb thrust engine was initially chosen to power the de Havilland DH 121 three-engined airliner for BEA. But as the power output rose, it was pronounced too great for its purpose by an airline concerned about a fall in passenger numbers. The DH 121 was reduced in size and the Medway was later cancelled. Some aspects of its design, however, were incorporated in the smaller RB.163. The basic design was completed in September 1958, and BEA signed a firm order for 24 of the revised airliner – later known as the Trident – powered by the Spey. BAC, however, was working from a different direction when it decided the Spey would be the ideal power plant for the enlarged Hunting/BAC H.107.

The prototype One-Eleven was powered by Spey Mk 505-14 engines, as were the two further flight test aircraft. They were later fitted with the more powerful Mk 506-14AW ('A' for small turbine and 'W' for water injection), as were some of the initial production aircraft. Most Series 200s had Mk 506-14s generating 10,410lbs of thrust with larger turbines. Those incorporating water injection – water was spayed into the combustion chambers for operations from hot and high airports – carried the 'W' designation.

The Aeroplane reported that BUA's 'worst case scenario' for operations outside Europe was the 815-mile sector between Ndola in what is now Zambia and Entebbe, Uganda. 'Ndola lies 4,160ft above sea level with a temperature of 26.5 degrees C and a runway length of 6,650ft,' the journal reported. 'The proposal for a water injection version of the Spey met this case'. As it happened, BUA never operated the One-Eleven on its East African network, although it did fly them in West Africa.

The Spey 25 Mark 511-14s fitted to Series 300 and 400 One-Elevens, as well as a few Series 200s, offered 11,400lbs of thrust. The heavier 510s ordered by BEA had 12,000lb of thrust, while all other 500s and 475s were powered by Spey 25 Mk 512-14DWs, generating 12,550lb of thrust.

Because the Spey had been designed for the Trident, the One-Eleven was able to incorporate its pods and engine installations. Thrust reversers were fitted to all versions of the One-Eleven and hush-kits were incorporated on all aircraft from 1976 onwards as well as being retro-fitted to most early examples.

The Spey also powered the Fokker F28 airliner, and military versions were specified for the Buccaneer naval strike fighter and British F.4 Phantom fighters. It was also used by the Nimrod maritime patrol aircraft, which was phased out of RAF service in 2011.

Chapter 4

The One-Eleven Takes Off

The crowds had been gathering since early morning. It would be a long wait and a wet one too, as heavy storms had been lashing the runway at Bournemouth's Hurn Airport for hours.

Despite the weather, Tuesday 20 August 1963 was an important day for the British aviation industry. It marked the first flight of a new airliner which the press was calling the 'bus-stop jet'.

At around 1400hrs, the aircraft made a slow-speed taxi run, but there was a delay as a brake unit was changed. There were further runs in the early evening. They were much faster. The aircraft's nose actually lifted and reverse thrust was applied for the first time. It then returned to its hangar to allow a snowplough to disperse the rainwater from the runway.

BAC's chief test pilot Jock Bryce and his deputy, Mike Lithgow, declared conditions suitable, and, as BAC managing director, Sir George Edwards, and members of the design team chatted nervously as the

The Prototype One-Eleven takes a break in its flight test schedule to pay its first visit to Luton on 12 September 1963, three weeks after the first flight. The caption to this Hunting Aircraft photograph points out that the visit was witnessed by almost every employee of the company 'in which the original idea of the One-Eleven was conceived'. It adds: 'A crowd, about 2,000 strong, swarmed enthusiastically round the aircraft after it had taxied in'. The One-Eleven departed after about 30 minutes in company with the Jet Provost chase aircraft. (Brooklands Aviation Museum, courtesy of BAE Systems)

It's just after 2000hrs and the first One-Eleven lands after a successful first flight with BAC's chief test pilot Jock Bryce and deputy Mike Lithgow on the flight deck. At the end of its 26-minute flight, the aircraft, registered G-ASHG, is accompanied by the Jet Provost chase aircraft.

Jet Provost chase aircraft took off. The One-Eleven prototype, painted in the dark blue and white livery of launch customer BUA and with a union flag displayed on the tail, began its take-off run.

G-ASHG took to the air at 1942hrs after a run of about 3,150ft. Accompanied by the Jet Provost piloted by 'Ollie' Oliver, the One-Eleven prototype reached a speed of 220mph and a height of 8,000ft. It was a short flight. The light was starting to fade when, at 2000hrs, the aircraft returned to Hurn with the chase plane in formation on its left wing. The aircraft touched down at 2008hrs after a brief 26-minute flight during which its undercarriage remained in the down position.

At the subsequent press conference, Bryce praised the aircraft's ease of handling. 'Rarely,' observed *Flight*, 'has a new aircraft taken to the air backed with so much commercial hope'. With 60 orders for the BAC One-Eleven, including an unprecedented number from American airlines, this was certainly true.

To *The Aeroplane*, it was the icing on the cake. The year had been notable for the progress made by four new British jet transports, the VC10, the Trident, the Hawker Siddeley 125 and the One-Eleven. 'All are at the flight test stage and no fewer than 179 of them have been ordered,' the journal noted, '66 by customers overseas'. It was 'a feather in any manufacturer's cap when 60 units can be sold off the drawing board before the first flight of the prototype'. *The Aeroplane* added optimistically: 'As the nearest competitor is many months behind it is reasonable to expect steady sales for the One-Eleven and its variants for years ahead'.

Survey of operators

Before the launch, a BAC market survey of around 100 operators indicated probable sales of 144 aircraft with up to 1,000 as a possibility. Edwards said he would be happy with the 400 achieved by the Viscount. His three-week visit confirmed that the best prospects were in the US.

The first US airline to sign up for the One-Eleven was the Texas-based Braniff International whose president, Chuck Beard, had already confided to Edwards' wife, Dinah, during their visit that he planned to do something he had never done before. He was about to place a big order for a British-built aircraft.

Accordingly, in October 1961, Braniff ordered six One-Eleven Series 200s with options on a further six. The order was later increased to 14. It was the first time a US carrier had ordered a British aircraft off the drawing board. Soon afterwards, US regional operator Mohawk Airlines announced an order for four with options on four more. This order was placed after the US Civil Aeronautics Bureau (CAB), which subsidised Mohawk, questioned the need for the carrier to operate jets, but its airline countered with figures showing that the One-Eleven's operating costs were 'substantially below' the piston-engined types it was currently using.

But two other US carriers, Ozark Airlines and Frontier Airlines, found their intentions to order a combined total of 11 One-Elevens blocked by CAB on the grounds that bigger subsidies would be required for the jets. Both carriers later operated DC-9s.

There were no such difficulties for one of America's big four airlines. Again, personal contact as well as confidence in BAC's after-sales service were key reasons for entering the name of American Airlines in the One-Eleven customer register. Another was the availability of an up-rated Spey engine with increased thrust, which enabled BAC to offer American the Series 400 with its ability to carry up to 89 passengers over longer stage lengths.

In July 1963, after persistent sales visits to American's New York headquarters by Geoffrey Knight and his sales teams, as well as by Edwards himself, the airline announced plans to buy 15 Series 400s,

BAC's chief test pilot appears calm as a microphone is thrust under his nose on 20 August 1963, the day he took the prototype One-Eleven for its first flight. Bryce told the waiting reporters that everything had gone according to plan. 'We flew to 8,000 feet and didn't exceed 180 knots,' he added. (Brooklands Museum, courtesy of BAE Systems)

It is getting dark as BAC's chief test pilot Jock Bryce descends from the prototype after its maiden flight to applause from BAC employees. (Brooklands Museum, courtesy of BAE Systems)

an order that was later increased to 30. Valued at US$40m, it was one of Britain's biggest single dollar export orders. Closer to home, another British independent, British Eagle, ordered an initial five and the Irish flag carrier Aer Lingus, four. Further overseas orders came from Philippine Airlines and Aloha Airlines of Hawaii.

No doubt it was this success that had so excited the press. Within days of the One-Eleven's first flight, *Flight* was reporting: 'Not only have Britain's national newspapers made big front page headlines out of it but some have printed leading articles also, drawing attention to the significance and importance of this uncommonly promising British product'.

It was just after the prototype's roll-out, on 28 July, that the journal published its own tribute. 'Perhaps' it noted in an editorial, 'BAC's own description of the One-Eleven as a jet successor to the Viscount, 200 mph faster with lower operating cost, sums it up best. Of all the new transport aircraft at present on offer, few appear to have brighter prospects than the One-Eleven'.

The first flight was also a notable achievement for BUA. *Flight* reported that the airline had played a major role 'in getting the project started with a time advantage that has helped in its sweeping sales success'. BUA's managing director Freddie Laker announced plans to introduce the One Eleven on its London–Genoa route by late summer 1964.

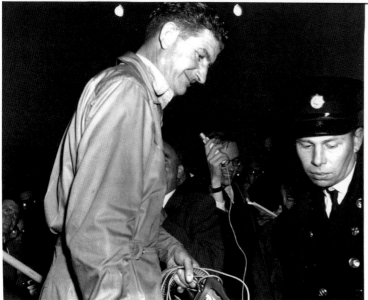

Above: The flight test crew who took the prototype BAC One-Eleven for its maiden outing are pictured here at the aircraft's roll-out at Hurn on 28 July 1963. They are (left to right): deputy chief test pilot Mike Lithgow, flight test observers Tony Neve and Dick Wright, and chief test pilot Jock Bryce. Lithgow and Wright were killed when the aircraft crashed in October. (BAE SYSTEMS Heritage)

Left: Jock Bryce's expression shows satisfaction as he leaves the One-Eleven after its first flight. Now he has to face the press. (Brooklands Museum, courtesy of BAE Systems)

The prototype One-Eleven returns to Hurn after its brief but successful maiden flight.

Loss of the prototype

After its maiden flight G-ASHG was moved to Wisley, which had been designated the One-Eleven flight test centre. It was a challenging programme, but in just over two months the prototype had completed 52 flights. Then came tragedy. On 22 October, the aircraft crashed near Cricklade, Wiltshire, with the loss of all on board, including Mike Lithgow, his co-pilot Dickie Rymer and flight test observer Dick Wright, who had also been on board during the first flight.

'It was one of the worst days of my life,' Edwards recalled. But there was no mystery about what had happened. When the flight data recorders were recovered after the accident, they revealed that up to the moment of impact the aircraft's forward speed had been very low and the rate of descent very high. It had hit the ground flat, in a horizontal attitude.

Lithgow and his crew had been conducting a series of stalling trials and, with eight degrees of wing flap and the centre of gravity in the furthest aft position, G-ASHG had failed to recover from a deep stall. The accident had been a clear indication of the dangers inherent in rear-engined T-tailed aircraft. It was evident that the aircraft could stall when the attitude of the wings blocked the flow of air over the tail and to the engines.

Once this had been understood, a 'fix' was quickly incorporated into the design. This entailed modifications to the wing leading edge to give more downward pitch at the stall, the incorporation of fully powered elevator controls and an electro-pneumatic stick pusher for use by the flight crew. As an additional safeguard, a tail parachute was fitted to the other One-Elevens in the test programme to assist with stall recovery.

BUA's second One-Eleven, G-ASJB, flew for the first time in February 1964 but crashed at Wisley the following month. Plans to rebuild it were subsequently abandoned. Note the tail-mounted parachute intended to prevent a recurrence of the accident in which the prototype was lost.

Another view of the prototype BAC One-Eleven following its first flight at Hurn on 20 August 1963. (BAE SYSTEMS Heritage)

The loss of G-ASHG and the following publicity was tragic, if not fatal, to the One-Eleven programme. It cannot have helped at a critical time. It is believed that it cost sales and the damage to its reputation no doubt helped Douglas and Boeing to make up ground with their DC-9 and 737, both of which had been launched after the One-Eleven.

A further set-back came in 1964 with a change of government. The cancellation of TSR.2 by the incoming Labour administration created financial difficulties for both BAC and the One-Eleven programme. In January 1965, Edwards wrote to aviation minister Roy Jenkins to express concern about the effect of the cancellation on One-Eleven customers, particularly American Airlines, who were feeling 'rather apprehensive'.

But American did not cancel its order. In any case, by that time, the One-Eleven had already entered passenger service.

JOCK BRYCE

Gabe Robb 'Jock' Bryce was born in 1921. He joined the RAF as a direct entry sergeant and learned to fly at Prestwick. He flew Blenheims and later Wellingtons before being commissioned and posted to the North Atlantic ferry force. After service in the Far East, Bryce returned to Britain in 1946 and the King's Flight at RAF Benson where he flew Vickers Vikings.

Demobilised in 1946, Bryce joined Vickers-Armstrongs (Aircraft) at Brooklands and Wisley as a test pilot. When 'Mutt' Summers retired, Bryce became chief test pilot. During his time at Vickers, Bryce was either captain or co-pilot on the first flight of 11 of the company's prototype aircraft, including the Viscount (Series 630, 700 and 800), the Valiant jet bomber, the Vanguard and, in 1962, the VC10. It was after the VC10's maiden outing that Bryce declared: 'It was the best flight I've ever had in a VC10'.

The One-Eleven, which first flew in August 1963, was Bryce's last prototype. He retired from flying two years later and became sales director (operations) at Weybridge. When he retired from BAC, he worked as vice-president (corporate aircraft sales) at the company's Washington, DC office. During this time, the One-Eleven was adopted as a corporate transport by several large corporations, including Tenneco and the Ford Motor Company.

MIKE LITHGOW

As one of Britain's best-known test pilots of the 1950s, Michael John Lithgow was a hero to a multitude of teenagers in a decade that saw the appearance of many exciting new prototypes. One of them was the Supermarine Swift jet fighter, and as chief test pilot of Vickers Supermarine, Lithgow achieved lasting fame by setting a new world air speed record.

He was born in 1920 and served with the Fleet Air Arm between 1939 and 1945. He flew Swordfish and Albacore torpedo bombers and later became a test pilot. At one point, he was stationed at the US Naval Air Test Center at Patuxent Field, Maryland. He left the navy with the rank of lieutenant commander and joined Vickers' Supermarine division in 1946, becoming chief test pilot two years later.

In September 1953, Lithgow gained lasting fame, when, in the Swift F.4 prototype, he flashed over the Libyan desert at a height of just 50ft to a record speed of 753.7 mph. A decade later, as a BAC test pilot, Lithgow accompanied Bryce on the One-Eleven's first flight, but in October 1963, he was killed when the same aircraft failed to recover from a deep stall and crashed near Cricklade, Wiltshire. Six other BAC flight test team members died with him.

Chapter 5

Into Service

The first One-Eleven service was commanded by BUA's fleet captain Stanley Websper. His crew comprised a first officer and three cabin staff. Also on board were the airline's managing director, Freddie Laker, and Lord Douglas of Kirtleside, a former BEA chairman who was now chairman of Horizon Holidays, a major tour operator client of BUA.

The One-Eleven had been chosen to replace Viscounts on the service, and BUA announced plans to operate six flights a week on the route in competition with Alitalia's Viscounts. Scheduled operations to Malaga and Barcelona were due to start later in the month followed by Amsterdam and Rotterdam, Seville, Tenerife and Las Palmas in spring and early summer. Next on the schedule were West African routes in June or July. The new jet would also be used for inclusive tour holiday flights 'to numerous European holiday destinations during 1965'.

London's Gatwick airport, 9 April 1965, and the first ever BAC One-Eleven commercial flight is boarding. The passengers preparing to mount the steps appear to be outnumbered by cameramen in this BUA photograph. The sharp-eyed will note Captain Stanley Websper glancing out of the left-hand flight deck window. And is that BUA managing director Freddie Laker waiting at the top of the steps to welcome the passengers for the inaugural British United Airways jet service to Genoa?

Three further One-Elevens would be delivered to BUA in April, with the remainder of the order following by early November. One of the aircraft from the original order for ten was, however, scrapped after an accident at Wisley in March, while the fourth production aircraft was rebuilt after a crash landing.

Deliveries soon fell behind schedule. Laker had expected that BUA would have all its aircraft by summer 1964 and had hoped to start the first services by the end of the year. After intensive flight testing and route-roving programmes, the One-Eleven was granted its Certificate of Airworthiness on 5 April after a 200-hour intensive route-proving programme.

Domestic services

On 4 January 1966, BUA introduced its domestic Interjet service from Gatwick to Glasgow, Edinburgh and Belfast. 'The One-Eleven was the first jet to operate on the domestic trunk routes from London,' recalls Stuart Hulse, who was BUA's public relations manager. 'They operated from Gatwick where the airline contributed over half the airport's traffic and reduced the flying time compared to BEA's

Braniff's first One-Eleven is about to be formally handed over to the airline in this publicity shot. N1541 made its maiden flight in June 1964 but is displaying the temporary registration G-ASUF. The Texan carrier launched its One-Eleven operations in April 1965. (BAE SYSTEMS Heritage)

Vanguard turboprops from Heathrow'. Indeed, BUA's One-Elevens, configured with between 69 and 74 seats, were proving popular with passengers. Load factors were encouraging, and eventually twice-daily services were offered on all Interjet routes.

Braniff's first One-Eleven (registered N1543) was handed over in March 1965 and received Federal Aviation Administration (FAA) type certification the following month. On 25 April, the airline inaugurated its One-Eleven operations with a multi-stop service from Corpus Christie, Texas, to Minneapolis-St Paul, Minnesota. The airline planned to work its One-Elevens hard. Turnaround times averaged 35 minutes. A typical daily schedule flown between 0825hrs and 1725hrs was Dallas–Lubbock–Amarillo–Lubbock–Dallas–Houston–Dallas–Lubbock–Dallas. Typical sector lengths varied between 112 and 300 miles. The shortest was the 67-mile hop between San Antonio and Austin.

As *The Aeroplane* noted: 'In the US the environmental conditions of the Braniff network were extremely demanding and had, like those of American Airlines, a considerable influence on the overall design performance of the One-Eleven as these were evolved'.

The third operator to start services with the new jet in 1965 was Aer Lingus. Its Dublin–Cork–Paris service was inaugurated on 6 June (with EI-ANE) and followed a six-day promotional tour of Europe.

Aer Lingus' first One-Eleven, EI-ANE, is rolled out at Hurn in March 1965. The Irish carrier ordered four of the short-haul jets, and 'ANE was delivered the following May. (BAE SYSTEMS Heritage)

This dramatic nose-on shot of an American Airlines One-Eleven Series 400 clearly shows that the type was known as the Astrojet in the carrier's service. American's order for 30 One-Elevens was worth a total of US$85m. (BAE SYSTEMS Heritage)

The One-Eleven was considered too small for the carrier's thicker short-haul routes such as Dublin–London and was used on services from Eire to UK destinations such as Manchester and Liverpool. Aer Lingus also used One-Elevens for IT operations, but although it remained a One-Eleven operator until 1991, its search for a bigger short-haul aircraft led it to order Boeing 737s.

Second US operator

On 15 July 1965, Mohawk became the second US airline to launch One-Eleven services. The largest US regional airline was delighted with its new jets. In particular, it appreciated the features that aided quick turnarounds, which were estimated to save it US$35,000 and one staff member per aircraft annually. In fact, it was able to manage a through stop with the One-Eleven of just six minutes, during which time it could disembark 64 passengers and board 47. Mohawk calculated that the One-Eleven's productivity was such that it could schedule three jet flights for every one by piston-engine Convairs.

Mohawk was acquired by Allegheny Airlines in 1971 and its One-Elevens flew on in the new livery alongside the carrier's DC-9s. Allegheny increased its One-Eleven fleet in 1972 with the addition of eight ex-Braniff aircraft. It subsequently changed its name to US Air and continued to operate One-Elevens until 1989.

American Airlines accepted delivery of its first One-Elevens in December 1965, and it took a year for all 30 to be handed over. All told, over 200 pilots were trained to operate the aircraft. The first crews took part in an intensive familiarisation programme in the last week of February 1966 during which 13 destinations on the airline's route network were visited.

American Airlines called the One-Eleven the 400 Astrojet and the first service was flown on the New York–Toronto route on 6 March followed by New York–Syracuse, where its One-Elevens were in

There was a spectacular ceremony to mark the roll-out at Hurn of Mohawk Airlines' first One-Eleven. The American regional carrier initially ordered four Series 200 aircraft and introduced them to its busy commuter routes to New York in July 1965. (BAE SYSTEMS Heritage)

A passenger in a hurry checks his watch as he leaves a British Eagle One-Eleven Series 200 at Glasgow Airport in the late 1960s. The British independent airline founded by Harold Bamberg received its first One-Elevens in the summer of 1966; it called them Super Jets and operated on UK domestic routes in competition with BEA's turboprop Vanguards. G-ATTP was originally ordered by Central African Airways but not delivered to the Rhodesian carrier because of post-UDI sanctions. British Eagle christened it *Swift*.

A pair of BUA One-Eleven Series 200s share the Gatwick apron in this photograph dated January 1970. The aircraft in the foreground, G-ASJD, was delivered in August 1965, while its sister-ship, G-ASJG, joined the fleet in July.

competition with Mohawk's Series 200s. By the end of American's first month of Astrojet operations, with 15 of its aircraft in service, the airline was able to report that there had been no technical delays with them. In 1967, American used its One-Elevens to try and regain market share lost to Eastern Airlines' no-reservation shuttle service between New York and Washington and Boston. Jet Express was inaugurated in February and quickly achieved load factors of 70 per cent with an hourly service, bookable seats and first-class options. In two years, the One-Elevens boosted American's traffic on the New York–Boston route more than five-fold.

BUA was not the first independent airliner to offer domestic services using turbine-powered aircraft, as British Eagle had operated Britannias and Viscounts in 1963. The same airline introduced jets three years later after taking delivery of two Series 207 aircraft originally ordered by Central African Airways. Due to sanctions against Rhodesia, following its unilateral declaration of independence, the aircraft were sold to Zambia Airways and immediately leased to British Eagle. On 9 May 1966, the airline inaugurated its One-Eleven Superjet service between London's Heathrow airport and Glasgow. That year, British Eagle received five One-Elevens, three of them Series 300s.

BUA kept its One-Elevens busy and used them for holiday charter flights as well as scheduled operations. Here, one of the airline's Series 500s, G-AWYS, is pictured disembarking 108 passengers bound for Elba at Pisa airport in August 1969.

Nice colour shot of a BUA One-Eleven as it cruises serenely above the clouds.

BRITISH UNITED AIRWAYS

The birth of British United Airways was the culmination of a process of airline consolidation that had been taking place during the 1950s. By the end of the decade, two airlines, Airwork and Hunting-Clan, dominated the private sector, but in no way could they be seen as independent counterweights to the two state-owned carriers.

The merger of Airwork and the aviation interests of Hunting-Clan was encouraged by aviation minister Duncan Sandys, the man whose 1957 defence policy had launched the process of consolidation within the manufacturing sector.

The new owner was a group of shipping companies and, although the actual make-up altered during BUA's lifetime, the Cayzer family's British and Commonwealth Shipping Company remained dominant. Sir Nicholas Cayzer and his cousin the Hon Anthony Cayzer were appointed to BUA's board and Airwork's Sir Myles Wyatt became chairman with Freddie Laker as managing director.

BUA had inherited a mixed bag of 50 or so aircraft, including Douglas DC-3s, DC-4s and DC-6s, Vickers Viscounts and Bristol Britannias and one of Laker's first tasks was to modernise the fleet. With its 1961 order for ten BAC One-Elevens, BUA became the first independent to launch a major new aircraft type. Edwards acknowledged that Laker's order had set the ball rolling and guaranteed government development funding for the new jet.

BUA also ordered VC10s and Laker's insistence on a forward cargo door and an interchangeable passenger cabin made it well suited to BUA's mixed traffic operations in Africa and South America. Indeed, BUA had acquired BOAC's South American routes after the government refused to underwrite the corporation's losses. BUA's Gatwick–Santiago service became profitable after only three years.

The air transport business had been changing during the 1960s, thanks partly to the Conservative government's desire to introduce competition through a loosening of the regulatory straitjacket. BUA was awarded 12 of the 22 scheduled routes it applied for in 1961. One of them was Gatwick–Genoa.

But in 1965, Laker quit BUA to start his own airline after a disagreement with Wyatt. BUA struggled to find a suitable replacement for Laker until Alan Bristow arrived in 1968. By that time, a deteriorating national economy had produced a harsher operating climate and Bristow was forced to slim the airline down.

When the government appointed a committee of inquiry to consider Britain's air transport industry in the 1970s, there was much talk of creating a 'second force' airline to balance the corporations' power. Although BUA's management saw their airline in this role, the Cayzer family began talks with the ambitious Scottish charter airline Caledonian Airways. Behind the scenes, though, the family was also talking to BOAC. When the negotiations with the state-owned airline were publicly revealed, Caledonian boss Adam Thomson adroitly outmanoeuvred the Cayzers by mobilising political support for a take-over of BUA.

In 1970, the merger became reality when Caledonian acquired BUA apart from its British United Island Airways operator, which remained in Cayzer family ownership. The merged airline was renamed British Caledonian Airways. Included in the deal were eight Series 200 One-Elevens, to which the new airline's golden lion logo on blue was applied to their tails. Two Series 500s were ordered after the merger was completed and additional aircraft were leased-in to meet short-term needs.

BRANIFF INTERNATIONAL AIRWAYS

Braniff Airways was launched in 1929 by Paul Revere Braniff, a World War One US Army Air Corps mechanic turned pilot. His brother, Tom, who had put up the cash, became president with Paul in charge of operations. By 1934, the airline was deeply in debt, but Paul secured a government airmail contract, flying mail between Chicago and Kansas City. Six months later, the airline started passenger services on the route.

The fleet grew rapidly with seven brand new Lockheed Electras, two Ford Tri-Motors and four Lockheed Vegas. Braniff put the Douglas DC-2 into service in 1937, with the first DC-3 arriving two years later. Hostesses were now employed to look after the passengers, although only ten out of 800 applicants were actually chosen. All were registered nurses, and they also had to be fluent in Spanish as the airline was flying from its Fort Worth hub to Mexico City, as well as to Kansas City and Chicago.

During World War Two, Braniff leased part of its fleet to the US military together with facilities for training pilots and engineers. When the war ended, Braniff regained control of a fleet that now included war-surplus DC-4s. As the post-war economy expanded, so too did Braniff's traffic and income. In 1946, Braniff gained permission to serve destinations in the Caribbean and Central and South America to end Pan Am's local monopoly.

Braniff continued its expansion in Latin America, but in 1954, Tom Braniff was killed in an aircraft accident and head of operations Charles 'Chuck' Beard assumed the presidency. The airline was consistently profitable under Beard's leadership, and it became the world's tenth biggest airline, but in 1964 it was sold to the Greatamerica Corporation. Harding Lawrence was appointed president.

It was Lawrence's wife, Mary, who conceived the spectacular makeover known as 'the end of the plain plane'. The aircraft appeared in seven bright colours, but there were also cabin crew uniforms styled by a top Italian fashion designer, glitzy gate rooms, jazzed-up ticket offices and a lavish corporate headquarters.

It was one of the airline's One-Elevens that was chosen to preview the new colours for the airline's board. It had been painted in orange and white to spearhead the transformation of a rather staid airline into the most innovative, colourful and sexy outfit in the business.

There was also a fresh wardrobe for flight attendants. Patti Stiffler, who joined Braniff in 1961, has vivid memories of the new uniform and of what passengers called 'the Braniff strip'. She recalls: 'They were mesmerised by it. There were several layers which we took off to work during the flight, starting with the jacket. There was a silver apron over the blouse. Purple bloomers formed the final layer. Before landing you had to put it all on again. We also had a reversible coat, orange on one side and purple on the other'.

The ensemble was topped by a plastic bubble rain hat that made the wearer look as though she had stepped out of a '60s sci-fi movie. 'It was a two-piece affair which zipped together,' Stiffler says. 'They were most uncomfortable and we didn't need them because there were jetways at most airports. There was no place on the airplane to store them. They were too big for the overhead lockers and the only other place was on the seats. Several of the girls pointed this out and they were dropped'.

Braniff expanded into Europe and Asia and had even become an operator of the Concorde supersonic airliner, although the SSTs flew subsonic between Dallas and Washington where they reverted to Air France or British Airways. But by the early 1980s, load factors were falling and Braniff was haemorrhaging cash. Debts topped U$740m when it filed for bankruptcy in 1982. There were several attempts to relaunch the airline, but all failed.

Chapter 6

Stretching the One-Eleven

I n January 1967, BEA's chairman Sir Anthony Milward and BAC's chairman and managing director Sir George Edwards signed a £32m contract to supply 18 examples of a new and bigger One-Eleven.

At Farnborough, G-AVML, resplendent in BEA livery, took part in the flying display. Later, Milward's wife Freida officially christened the variant Super One-Eleven. The name had been chosen from nearly 900 entries submitted by BEA and BAC staff.

The airline had ordered its aircraft in a 97-seat single-class cabin configuration, and according to BEA's publicity, 'The light, bright spacious interior of the Super One-Eleven helps make it a brilliant new addition to BEA's jetliner fleet'. The launch of the One-Eleven Series 500 followed the government's agreement to contribute the £9m development costs, which were, as usual, to be repaid by a levy on sales.

With the bigger variant accounting for 38 per cent of all One-Eleven sales, it was clearly a significant development, if not quite the turning point that it had been hailed at the time. BAC had proposed a stretched One-Eleven back in 1963. The size and capacity of the baseline Series 200 had reflected the

market going into the 1960s, rather than the growth recorded during the decade's first half. American competition in the shape of the Douglas DC-9 and the Boeing 737 had seemed to be lagging behind Europe. Indeed, the French Sud Caravelle and the One-Eleven appeared to have stolen a march on them.

Boeing launches 737

The success of the European designs had influenced Boeing in its decision to launch a short-haul jet, but when the company finally did so in February 1965 it was clear that its 737 was in a different league. The Seattle-based manufacturer had designed its newest jet around the fuselage cross-section of its earlier 707 and 727 models. This resulted in a six-abreast seating layout and produced increased range and payload. Boeing had, like Douglas, chosen the Pratt & Whitney JT8D engine, which in the 737 offered 3,000lb more thrust than the One-Eleven's Speys.

Three days after the 737's launch, Lufthansa ordered 21 of the initial -100 version, and by April, Boeing had announced a stretched version. It was this 124-seat 737-200 that particularly appealed to Britannia Airways. Late in 1965, BAC offered a 92-passenger One-Eleven Series 400 to the British charter airline, but it was rejected, to the fury of the British press and the consternation of the government.

Despite the pressure, Britannia became the first European carrier to receive 737-200s despite having to pay 14 per cent import duty on them. And it was not the only airline to be frustrated by BAC's inability to offer a bigger One-Eleven. Both Aer Lingus, which wanted a larger capacity aircraft for its Dublin–London service, and Air France became 737 operators. These events, together with predictions

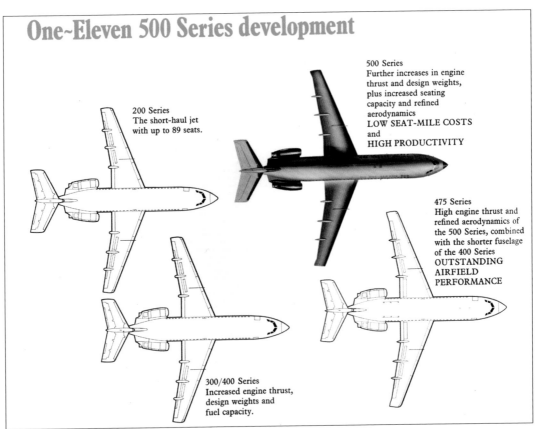

One~Eleven 500 Series development

200 Series
The short-haul jet with up to 89 seats.

500 Series
Further increases in engine thrust and design weights, plus increased seating capacity and refined aerodynamics
LOW SEAT-MILE COSTS and
HIGH PRODUCTIVITY

475 Series
High engine thrust and refined aerodynamics of the 500 Series, combined with the shorter fuselage of the 400 Series
OUTSTANDING AIRFIELD PERFORMANCE

300/400 Series
Increased engine thrust, design weights and fuel capacity.

BEA's Super One-Elevens differed from other Series 500s in having avionics supplied by Smiths Industries to provide commonality with the airline's Tridents. The cost of the modifications prompted BAC's chief test pilot Brian Trubshaw to claim it would almost be enough to buy another One-Eleven! (BAE SYSTEMS Heritage)

This pair of Series 500s display the livery of Caledonian Airways. The Scottish-based charter carrier ordered four One-Elevens before its merger with BUA in 1970 to form British Caledonian Airways. G-AWWY was the second aircraft to be delivered, joining the fleet in March 1969, while 'WZ arrived the following month. (BAE SYSTEMS Heritage)

of strong traffic growth, prompted BAC to look again at stretching the One-Eleven, especially as BEA was now looking for a replacement for its Viscounts.

For some time, BAC had been pressing Rolls-Royce to squeeze more power from the Spey, and now, in 1966, the need was becoming more urgent as BEA began to show interest in an aircraft it had previously ignored. Studies indicated that a relatively modest increase in maximum take-off weight would be required to meet BEA's needs. The Rolls-Royce Spey Mk 512 offered 10 per cent more thrust compared with the Mk 511 that powered the Series 400.

The way was now clear for a modest stretch of the One-Eleven, except that the government was delaying its decision on launch aid. BEA had previously indicated its desire to follow Britannia and buy the 737 as well as the 727. Ministers categorically refused to allow this. Matters were complicated by the airline asking for a financial restructuring to compensate it for being forced to buy British.

Both the airline and the government came under strong criticism. Ministers were attacked for allowing the argument to be conducted in public to the detriment of the One-Eleven's prospects in export markets. But during a House of Commons debate on the aircraft industry, which had been initiated by the Conservative opposition in November 1966, Douglas Jay, President of the Board of Trade, said he was anxious to avoid delaying BEA's re-equipment with British jets.

Jay disclosed that, less than a month earlier, Milward had told him 'for the first time' that BEA wanted to buy the Series 500. Jay noted that Milward had described the aircraft as having 'very attractive economic possibilities'. Jay added: 'I believe this new One-Eleven has excellent export prospects as well as being highly suitable for BEA. With adequate load facilities these new aircraft may

British Midland Airways acquired three 119-seat Series 523s early in 1970 intending to use them on its scheduled and charter routes but found the aircraft unsuited to its operations and sold them by the end of 1974. G-AXLL, pictured here, eventually operated in European Aviation Air Charter livery before being sold to Nigeria.

The Boeing 737 was launched in early 1965 with an order from Lufthansa. British charter carrier, Britannia Airways, wanted the bigger Series 200 version seating 117 and, in June 1967, ordered three despite government pressure to buy the One-Eleven instead. (Tom Singfield)

well prove to be commercially very attractive'. But the fact remained that Britain's short-haul flag carrier had demanded financial compensation for operating the One-Eleven. This was not lost on foreign airlines seeking a new short-haul jet or on Douglas and Boeing sales staff.

Series 500 launched

Work began at Wisley on the first Series 500 in February 1967. It was actually the Series 400 development aircraft, G-ASYD (construction number 053), which was cut into three to have two fuselage extensions installed, a 100in one behind the flight deck and a 62in plug behind the wings. The wing tips were also extended. The additions had been completed by the end of April so that, two months later and six weeks ahead of schedule, the aircraft was ready for its first flight.

'YD was, however, a conversion of an existing aircraft, and the first true Series 500 and BEA's first Series 510 was G-AVMH, which made its maiden flight in February 1968. This aircraft incorporated the equipment changes required by BEA, which included replacing the Collins avionics suite with Smiths equipment to produce a flight deck similar to that of the Trident. BEA had, however, agreed that the three-crew cockpit to which it had previously been committed with its Comet 4Bs and Tridents was not necessary. The One-Eleven had successfully demonstrated several years of two-crew operations. BAC test pilot Brian Trubshaw claimed that the changes insisted upon by BEA had almost doubled the cost of its One-Elevens.

By July, BEA's second aircraft, G-AVMI, was ready for the start of crew training and a month later the Series 500 received certification. The stretched One-Eleven was ready for operations but its chief rival, the DC-9-30, had already been in service for 18 months. This indicated how far BAC's early lead over the competition had been eroded.

In November, BEA introduced the One-Eleven into scheduled service on its internal German routes. It was also launched on the Manchester–London route. The decision to base the new aircraft at Manchester reflected the need to win traffic between that city and the capital that had been lost to rail services following electrification. It also brought a morale boost for BEA staff at Manchester, who had felt themselves overshadowed for many years by their colleagues at Liverpool.

In a 1971 internal reorganisation, the Super One-Eleven division took over responsibility for all international services from Manchester and domestic operations apart from those to the Channel Islands. It also assumed responsibility for the German internal services. After nearly five years of unspectacular, trouble-free operations, all 18 Super One-Elevens continued to fly on in British Airways livery.

Meanwhile, seven aircraft had been delivered to BEA by the end of 1968, with all but one of the remainders being handed over the following year. G-AVMX was retained by BAC for Autoland trials until May 1970. As it happened, BEA was to operate more One-Elevens than the 18 Series 510s it originally ordered. By the time of its merger with BOAC to form British Airways in 1974, BEA had acquired a further seven aircraft, all Series 400s.

Right: The One-Eleven Series 475 was intended to operate in remote areas, and BAC tested the prototype at Waterbeach to enable the variant to be certificated for operation from unmade strips. Here, G-ASYD kicks up the dust during the early summer of 1972.

Below: British Airways' G-AVMW shares the apron with a pair of Viscounts, the aircraft the One-Eleven was designed to replace. 'MW was originally ordered by BEA, but all of the fleet had to be repainted to reflect the change brought about by the merger with BOAC. (BAE SYSTEMS Heritage)

More BA One-Elevens

In 1978, BA again sought permission to buy Boeing 737s. There was opposition from BAC and the trades unions, but this time the government gave in. The consolation prize for BAC and its workers was an order for a trio of One-Elevens, designated Series 539. They were delivered to the airline during 1980 but without the special equipment featured on the Series 510s. The last BA One-Eleven service was flown in 1993, although the type soldiered on with franchise partners until 1998.

BA also inherited 13 further Series 500s when it acquired BCal in 1987. Caledonian had ordered three Series 509s in 1969. It too had originally wanted Boeing 737s but deferred to government pressure as part of a deal in which the Scottish charter carrier was permitted to add 707s to its fleet. But former BCal communications director Tony Cocklin recalls: 'As it turned out, the 500 series was a fine aircraft and did a good job for the airline'.

BUA had ordered eight of the stretched One-Elevens, which joined the BCal fleet after the merger in 1970. At this time, the combined fleet comprised eight 201s and 12 Series 500s.

Other British Series 500 operators included British Midland Airways, which used its three 119-seater 523s on both scheduled and charter services, and Court Line. Although the operator, which called itself Britain's premier holiday airline, was relatively short-lived, Court Line had a dozen Series 500s. Its original 518 aircraft had the 119-seat configuration, the biggest applied to a One-Eleven.

These aircraft were used for intensive inclusive tour operations, but the airline collapsed spectacularly in August 1974 at the height of the holiday season. Its aircraft were returned to the manufacturers and various creditors and were soon passed to other operators. But the Court Line affair was to have lasting repercussions on the regulation of charter operations, with a system of financial protection for holidaymakers that continues to this day.

Left: **The Sud Caravelle introduced the rear-mounted engine location featured by the One-Eleven and the Douglas DC-9.**

THE HYBRID

If any One-Eleven led a busy and varied life, it was G-ASYD. In August 1967, it was the first of the stretched Series 500s to fly and less than three years later it was the first Series 475.

The new variant, essentially a short fuselage aircraft with Spey Mk 512s and the extended wings of the Series 500, was announced in January 1970. Intended for operation in more remote areas of the world, it offered better short field performance with new aerodynamic and structural features.

The main wheels had a diameter 4in bigger than those of the Series 500 and operated at lower tyre pressures. This meant a redesign of the main gear bays, doors and under-fuselage area. Deflectors were added to stop damage from thrown-up debris. Glass-fibre coating of the under-surfaces was offered as an extra. The result of these modifications was a jet with the field performance of a DC-3.

To become the prototype of the new variant, G-ASYD had the previously fitted fuselage extensions removed. The work was completed a month ahead of schedule, and the aircraft flew again for the first time at the end of August. Days later, it was on display at Farnborough. BAC made great efforts to demonstrate the aircraft's ability to operate from short fields. In addition to tests all over the world, including the Himalayas, BAC conducted a series of trials closer to home on a specially prepared rough field at Waterbeach, Cambridge.

In 1972, the second production Series 475, G-AZUK, undertook a two-week sales tour of South America, visiting four countries as well as airfields that had never before seen jets. Yet, despite all the hard work, BAC was to build just nine Series 475s. The first two were delivered to Faucett of Peru in 1971. The 74-seaters were operated into unpaved jungle runways in the Amazon and high up in the Andes. The aircraft were withdrawn after ten years of intensive use.

Chapter 7
Service Around the World

The independent operators that offered both scheduled services and holiday charter flights came to rely on the BAC One-Eleven. For two decades, airports like Gatwick and Luton seemed to be full them. Even Ryanair, which today calls itself Europe's premier low-cost airline, started its jet services with One-Elevens, having launched scheduled operations with HS748 turboprops.

British Eagle, British Island Airways, British Midland Airways, Caledonian (and later British Caledonian Airways), Channel Airways, Court Line, Dan-Air, Laker, Monarch – the list seems endless, but for a while the common factor was the One-Eleven. And they were usually worked hard in what was a highly competitive, not to say cutthroat, business.

During its relatively brief history, Court Line quickly gained a reputation for getting the best out of its equipment. It started as a shipping line that acquired an airline, Autair International, a small independent operator that had bought four new One-Eleven Series 400s. Although it had flown scheduled services, Autair had entered the charter business when Clarksons Holidays began using its aircraft to fly day-trippers to Rotterdam en route to the Dutch bulb fields.

The holiday charter airline Court Line operated a fleet of brightly coloured BAC One-Eleven 500s, including G-AXMH *Halcyon Sun*.

By 1969, Autair was carrying 500,000 charter passengers a year compared with 66,000 scheduled. The loss-making scheduled operations were phased out in favour of charters as Clarksons was now buying over 70 per cent of capacity. Then, on 1 January 1970, Autair became Court Line and the aircraft received new paint jobs in bright jelly-bean colour schemes.

Seven 119-seat Series 500s had been ordered to replace the 89-seat Series 400s. They received names incorporating the word 'Halcyon' starting with the pink-painted *Halcyon Breeze*. One of the airline's marketing staff, Chris Lockwood, was present at the aircraft's roll-out at Filton along with a group of journalists. He recalls: 'One of the BAC workers watching it emerge from the hangar said: "What are you going to do with that, mate, fly it or suck it?"' Inevitably, rival airlines had their own take on the colours, especially the pink-painted example. One pilot is reported to have asked ATC: 'Am I clear to land after the *Financial Times*?'

Seat back catering
Court Line believed its shipping experience enabled it to bring new ideas to the airline business. One of them was 'time charters,' a long-established concept in the oil tanker business. Another innovation was 'seat back catering'. This not only relieved the cabin crew of serving meals, but, by

Bahamas Airways ordered two BAC One-Eleven Series 500s, which it operated as Flamingo Jets. Here, VP-BCN and 'BCO show off their forward airstairs at Hurn before delivery in 1969. Although the airline ordered a third aircraft, it was not delivered.

One-Elevens continued to operate on US domestic routes into the late 1980s. Allegheny Airlines had acquired some of Mohawk's Series 200 aircraft as well as some of Braniff's during the 1970s and these aircraft passed to USAir on its formation.

British Eagle's One-Eleven G-ATTP Super Jet named *Swift* cruises above the clouds in this shot dated September 1966. The British independent used its aircraft on UK domestic routes and acquired this aircraft when it was diverted from Central African Airways, which had originally ordered it.

reducing the size of galleys, it also freed up space equivalent to three One-Eleven seats. Preprepared meals were packed into separate seat-back compartments, one for outbound passengers, the other for inbound.

It was, says Chris Lockwood, part of the airline's ruthless drive to cut costs. But the resulting hump in the seat back further reduced the already tight seat pitch. 'It wasn't popular. The meals were pretty dismal,' Lockwood recalls. 'There was no hot food so it was salad, maybe a pork pie, cake and biscuits and a plastic cup for tea or coffee'. The trouble was, though, that if outbound passengers were still hungry, they could eat the food intended for the inbound ones. 'There was a lock and the chief stewardess had the key,' Chris Lockwood recalls, 'but people soon worked out how to open them. A ball point pen would do it'.

Court Line acquired wide-bodied TriStars to supplement the One-Elevens but collapsed at the height of the 1974 summer season. Four of its Series 500s passed to Dan-Air, which was to operate a substantial fleet comprising all principal variants. Over the years, Dan-Air's One-Elevens were used for both schedule and charter services, and by the early 1980s these aircraft were flying six to seven sectors a day during the week and up to nine at weekends.

IT operations were not confined to Britain. German charter airline Panair International was owned by a major tour operator, and it eventually acquired four Series 500s for operations from its base at Dusseldorf. The airline went bust in 1971. Other German One-Eleven charter operators included Germanair and also Bavaria Flug, which was Germany's first One-Eleven operator with four Series 400s. The carrier also operated domestic services for Lufthansa and, despite losing one of its aircraft in 1970, Bavaria ordered three Series 500s.

Philippine Airlines was another loyal One-Eleven operator. It ordered its first Series 400s in 1966 and later acquired five Series 500s, the last of which was delivered in 1974. The One-Eleven was also widely used in Latin America. Austral of Argentina was the first customer with four Series 400s for domestic and international operations by both itself and ALA. Austral also bought Series 500s and continued operating them until 1994. Its last Series 400 was retired in 1988. Other Latin American Series 400 operators were TACA of El Salvador, LACSA of Costa Rica, LANICA of Nicaragua and VASP of Brazil. Aviateca of Guatemala was another Series 500 operator. In the Middle East, Gulf Air of Bahrain became the region's first One-Eleven user in 1969 when it received a Series 400.

The fact was that, after its first five years in service, the One-Eleven had become Britain's most successful airliner programme as well as the nation's premier dollar earner. A total of 27 airlines all over the world were operating the aircraft. Others were in use as corporate transports and the type had been adopted by several air forces.

As the second-hand market developed, One-Elevens began to appear all over the world. Lease arrangements saw them wearing the liveries of major airlines like KLM, SAS and Sabena. But perhaps the biggest single One-Eleven operator never to own a new example was Britain's Dan-Air, which owned 26, a mix of all major variants. The carrier acquired its first ex-American Airlines aircraft in March 1969 followed by a pair of Series 300s later in the year and early 1970.

Dan-Air's One-Elevens

When Dan-Air ceased operations and was absorbed by British Airways in 1992, Southend-based British Air Ferries acquired the entire fleet of Series 500s, a total of 11 aircraft. Only five were put into service. Another five were broken up for spares and one was sold to Nigeria, which gained a reputation as something of a One-Eleven graveyard.

Above: **Dan-Air operated all major One-Eleven variants even though it bought none of them new. The aircraft were used for both scheduled and non-scheduled holiday operations. Here, one of the carrier's aircraft shares the Luton ramp with a pair of Autair's Series 400, which were later repainted in Court Line livery. (BAE SYSTEMS Heritage)**

Right: **Like other independent One-Eleven operators, British Eagle used its aircraft for both scheduled and non-scheduled operations. G-ATTP *Swift* is pictured at Tunis' Carthage airport during the 1960s.**

The Ford Motor Company operated two One-Elevens, based at Stansted, to ferry personnel between its European sites.

Southend-based Channel Airways established by former Sqn Ldr Jack Jones was a pioneer of the British package holiday. It acquired three Series 400 One-Elevens and operated them in a high-density configuration. The aircraft were known as Continental Golden Jets to reflect their colour scheme. Pictured here is G-AVGP, which was delivered in June 1967 but quickly sold to Autair.

The BAF One-Elevens entered service in December 1992 in either a 119-seat single class or a 99-seat mixed class configuration. The airline was later renamed British World Airlines (BWA) and its operations moved to Stansted. A three-times weekly scheduled service from Stansted to Bucharest was launched in June 1993 but dropped the following March due to lack of traffic. The last of BWA's One-Elevens was withdrawn in 2000.

A Series 400 One-Eleven for Tarom pictured under construction at Hurn. The Romanian airline ordered six aircraft, the first of which, YR-BCA, first flew in January 1968. The last aircraft of the order was delivered in December 1969. (BAE SYSTEMS Heritage)

Luxurious interior of a corporate One-Eleven. (BAE SYSTEMS Heritage)

It is 26 January 1980, and the first fuselage from the Hurn production line is loaded into an Aeromaritime Super Guppy aircraft for the journey to Romania and the One-Eleven production line. (BAE SYSTEMS Heritage)

CORPORATE ONE-ELEVENS

The first of many corporate One-Elevens was ordered for Helmut Horten GmbH, a West German chain store operator, in June 1964. The Series 200 came with a £90,000 price tag and a 34-seat cabin. The aircraft, which was intended to transport the company's executives between its 46 stores, was delivered in January 1966 as a replacement for a turboprop Fokker F27.

Page Airways International was appointed US sales agent for executive One-Elevens in the US and it ordered two examples in November 1964. The first two US corporate clients were Tenneco, previously the Tennessee Gas Transmission Company, whose Series 200 was delivered in April 1966, and Victor Comptometer, which received a Series 400 in September 1966. Both companies had previously operated executive Viscounts.

Among operators of executive One-Elevens in Europe was the Ford Motor Company. It acquired two Series 400s from the Brazilian Air Force in December 1976 together with an ex-Bavaria/Germanair example the following November. All three were used to transport personnel between Ford's numerous production centres throughout Europe, and the first began a regular service between Stansted and Cologne in February 1977. Two of the aircraft were sold in Nigeria in 1993 while the third was sold in Indonesia.

One of the former South American Series 400s, equipped with a freight door and, reregistered as G-BGTU, was operated by Rolls-Royce. From its Filton base the aircraft carried freight and personnel to support its involvement in the Tornado and Eurofighter/Typhoon programmes. As a result, the aircraft flew a regular 16 sectors per week to Turbo Union partners in Munich and Turin with Madrid added in the 1990s.

A larger number of corporate One-Elevens were operated in the US, where many were inevitably ex-American Airlines, and in Saudi Arabia. Many of these aircraft were fitted with extra fuel tanks in the rear of the forward hold to give them trans-Atlantic capability.

ROMANIAN ONE-ELEVENS

Today Romania is a member of the European Union, but in the 1960s the country was part of the Soviet bloc. Yet, unlike most countries on that side of the Iron Curtain, Romania resisted pressure for its airlines to operate Soviet-built equipment. Indeed, its enthusiasm for British airliners led to plans for the manufacture of two different types in Bucharest.

It began when the Romanian national airline Tarom announced an order for six BAC One-Eleven Series 400s. Part of the deal was an off-set arrangement under which Romania would part-manufacture examples of the Britten-Norman Islander ten-seat transport, which would then be flown back to the Isle of Wight for furnishing.

Tarom's One-Elevens were delivered as 84 seaters between December 1968 and December 1969. They were supplemented by a further two second-hand examples bought from BAC. In the 1970s, Tarom was back with an order for five Series 500s, the first of which was delivered in March 1977. The deal involved the manufacture of further Islanders in Romania.

That year, BAC was amalgamated with Hawker Siddeley to form the nationalised British Aerospace. The government's decision to support the launch of the BAe 146 brought One-Eleven production in the UK to an end. Accordingly, the company saw an opportunity to continue manufacture in Romania and an agreement was reached during the state visit to Britain of the country's head of state, President Ceausescu, in the summer of 1978.

The agreement was valued at over £150m. The British company retained its design authority and comprehensive on-site supervision, which enabled completed aircraft to receive simultaneous certification by the British as well as Romanian authorities. The partnership was recognised by its name, which involved a contraction of Romania and BAC: Rombac.

The agreement for licensed production at the Romanian Government aircraft (IRMA) factory at Baneasa near Bucharest was signed in June 1979. As a first step towards the transfer of production, BAC produced two Series 525 passenger aircraft and a single windowless freighter Series 485. They were supplied as training aircraft. A further 22 One-Elevens were then to be supplied in kit form from the UK and assembled locally with gradually increasing Romanian content. An Aeromartime Guppy delivered the first complete fuselage from Hurn to Baneasa in January 1980, while Tradewinds CL-44s carried wings and other major components.

The first Rombac One-Eleven, a series 561RC, was rolled out at Baneasa on 27 August 1982 and flew for the first time in September 1982. But plans for the production of 80 One-Elevens in Romania were curtailed by political and social unrest. These problems were compounded by a lack of hard currency, which made it difficult to acquire even basic items. It was also reported that working conditions in the factory made life unpleasant for the workers, particularly during the winter when temperatures dropped to -25 degrees Celsius, too cold for paint and adhesives to be applied. Workers were often sent home when conditions got too bad.

In the end, only nine Series 561s were produced between September 1982 and April 1989. The first was delivered to Tarom at the end of December 1982. The Romanian carrier took delivery of all but two of the aircraft produced, with the remaining two going to Romavia, the last of which was delivered in January 1993. Two further aircraft were partially completed when production was abandoned and scrapped.

Tarom's One-Elevens were leased to many operators, including Dan-Air and British Island Airways, Loganair and London European in the UK as well as Ryanair, Lauda Air and several Yugoslav airlines. BAe officially terminated its agreement with Romaero in July 1993.

The third Romanian-built One-Eleven, registered YR-BRC, was exhibited at the 1984 SBAC show at Farnborough.

Chapter 8

Military Service

T he first One-Elevens to wear military markings were those ordered in December 1965 by the Royal Australian Air Force (RAAF). The two Series 217 aircraft were delivered in 1967 and 1968 and were distinguished by the use of the higher-powered Spey 511s of the 400 series. The use of water injection was intended to provide better performance in high-temperature operations. As well as their domestic transport duties with No 34 Squadron, the aircraft (A12-124 and A12-125) took part in extensive diplomatic tours of the Far East. The aircraft carried the Queen and Prince Philip. They were initially configured with two separate cabins seating 26 and 30 passengers, but this was later changed to a 28-seat layout. The aircraft were later bought by Paul Stoddert's European Aviation and sold on to Okada Air of Nigeria.

The Royal Australian Air Force ordered two One-Elevens for use as executive transports, one of which is pictured at Hurn. The aircraft were hybrids, essentially Series 200s with the up-rated engines of the Series 400. After a career transporting passengers as distinguished as the Queen and the Duke of Edinburgh, the aircraft were bought by UK-based Australian entrepreneur Paul Stoddart and formed the basis of the European Aviation operation. (BAE SYSTEMS Heritage)

Two Series 423s were delivered to the Brazilian Air Force between October 1968 and May 1969. They were fitted out by Marshalls of Cambridge as VIP transports with two separate cabins. One had an executive layout, while the other had 24 first-class style seats. They were operated on government and military business. The aircraft were later acquired by the Ford Motor Company. The Philippine Air Force also acquired an ex-Channel Airways Series 400 for use as a VIP transport operated by No 702 Squadron. This aircraft was withdrawn from service in 1984.

The longest serving military One-Elevens, however, were the Omani Series 485s, which were delivered between December 1974 and November 1975. The last remained in service until 2010. The three ordered by the Sultan of Oman's Air Force to replace its Vickers Viscounts were the only military Series 475s to be ordered new. Although their rough field performance was never actually tested, one of the One-Elevens made demonstration landings at a remote desert strip to prove its capabilities to senior officers.

Just three weeks after it was delivered, the third aircraft was severely damaged in a cockpit fire which broke out when the oxygen system was being replenished. The aircraft had to be shipped back to Hurn for repair. It was returned in February 1977. The second aircraft was also sent back to its manufacturer, to have a large freight door fitted, returning to service in August 1977. Long range tanks were later fitted to the first aircraft and over the years all three received updated avionics equipment.

The two One-Elevens ordered by the RAAF are pictured in a line-up at Hurn with aircraft destined for Bavaria Flug and VASP. (BAE SYSTEMS Heritage)

Three Series 485 aircraft were ordered for the Omani air force and proved to be the longest-serving military One-Elevens. They were delivered between December 1974 and November 1975 and the last remained in service until 2010.

The standard seating layout was 79, although the one equipped with long-range tanks was usually fitted with 59 seats. All three aircraft could have either flat or roller floors making them very adaptable. They were all used regularly for freight and medical relief flights as well as for regular services carrying military personnel and their families.

It was eventually decided to replace the One-Elevens with a trio of Airbus A320-214 VIP transports, the first of which was delivered in December 2008. This coincided with the withdrawal of the first One-Eleven, which had flown 22,253 hours and made 18,529 landings. The second went in 2009 after 29,571 hours and 24,543 landings, while the third was honoured with a commemorative fly-past to mark its last sortie in June 2010. It had flown 27,797 hours and completed 23,230 landings.

Experimental One-Elevens

The first British-operated One-Eleven to wear military markings was a Series 201, previously registered G-ASJD and bought from British Caledonian Airways in 1971. The aircraft was given the military serial XX105. Fitted with long-range tanks and specialist radar, it was delivered to the Blind Landing Experimental Unit at Thurleigh, Bedfordshire, in March 1973. It was subsequently relocated to Farnborough and then Boscombe Down to test civil and military avionics systems. In the 1990s, the aircraft tested future air traffic control procedures and systems for air traffic service provider NATS. In May 2003, this historic aircraft flew in a special formation with QinetiQ's two other remaining operational One-Elevens, before making its final flypast at Hurn the following month.

An ex-Philippine Airlines Series 402 was acquired for the Royal Aircraft Establishment, which used it for a variety of research programmes displaying the military serial XX919. Its duties included satellite communications and sonar-buoy research – with the rear stairwell used for launches – and trials of long-range navigation aids and aerials as well as high frequency communications equipment. From the 1980s, it was given a colourful paint scheme, and in 1990 it received a miniature tail-mounted TV camera and video system. The aircraft made its last flight in March in 1997 and was broken-up at Boscombe Down in 2000.

When one of the Omani One-Elevens suffered extensive damage in an accident, which happened as its oxygen system was being replenished, the aircraft was returned to its manufacturer for repairs. Here, its fuselage is trucked through the street of Bournemouth on its way to nearby Hurn. (BAE SYSTEMS Heritage)

Two Series 479s of Air Pacific were acquired in 1984. One became ZE433 and was based at Bedford where it was converted into a flying laboratory, with its nose extended to accommodate the Blue Vixen lightweight airborne interception radar, which was intended for installation in the Sea Harrier FA2. Later, the aircraft was further modified to accept the ECR90 radar for the Eurofighter Typhoon. Seating was installed for monitoring the tests. The aircraft was transferred to GEC Ferranti Defence Systems Ltd in 1984 and based at Edinburgh for radar and associated trials. The aircraft made its last flight, from Boscombe Down, in November 2008.

'Raspberry ripple'

The second ex-Air Pacific aircraft was acquired by the Empire Test Pilots' School as ZE432 and initially painted in the colourful 'raspberry ripple' scheme. Training stations were installed in the forward cabin while the standard airline seating and overhead racks were retained to the rear. The aircraft was withdrawn from service in November 2009 following the discovery of major airframe corrosion.

The final aircraft to wear red, white and blue roundels was built in 1980 as a Series 500. It was delivered to British Airways with the registration G-BGKE and used for domestic operations. Sold to GEC Marconi Defence Ltd in February 1991, the aircraft was leased to the Defence Research Agency, now QinetiQ. After a major overhaul, Kilo Echo was transferred to the Royal Aircraft Establishment, Bedford. It later received the military serial ZH763 and moved to Boscombe Down in July 1994.

What a big nose you've got! The modified One-Eleven operated by GEC Ferranti to test the ECR 90 radar for the Eurofighter Typhoon in its outsize nose radome prepares to make its first flight from its Edinburgh base.

Trials of enhanced surveillance radar were undertaken until 2002. Ownership was transferred to QinetiQ in January 2003, and the aircraft was progressively transformed to fulfil the flying laboratory role with the addition of a large removable belly radome and a side radome for radar trials work.

The trials and test equipment included a Honeywell military H764G ring laser gyro inertial navigation system with embedded GPS receiver and data bus output, integrated with a cockpit control and display navigation unit and a digital air data unit. The system interfaced with the aircraft's autopilot and auto-throttle to provide autonomous control during surrogate unmanned air vehicle trials. A stand-alone Garmin 165 GPS was also installed. To meet European Aviation Safety Agency requirements, an Allied Signal/Honeywell TCAS 2 and dual Mode S transponder system were also installed.

Retirement from QinetiQ

A series of successful flight trials were undertaken using QinetiQ's Tornado integrated avionics research aircraft (ZD902) flown by an RAF test pilot, with ZH763 acting as a surrogate unmanned air vehicle. Once both aircraft were airborne, the Tornado pilot assumed control of the 'BAC One-Eleven surrogate UAV' and three simulated UAVs during each flight. This aircraft was the last BAC One-Eleven to fly in the UK and was donated to a museum in 2013. It was replaced in QinetiQ's service by an Avro RJ100.

Although the One-Eleven was evaluated for the Queen's Flight of the RAF on several occasions, it was never actually adopted due to budgetary considerations. The type was considered with several

One-Elevens were proposed for the RAF's Queen's Flight on several occasions, and trials were actually conducted. This BAC artist's impression shows an aircraft in dedicated Queen's Flight livery. (BAE SYSTEMS Heritage)

In 1967, BAC proposed a Series 400 variant for casualty (CASEVAC) duties with the USAF's Military Airlift Command. This BAC model shows how it might have appeared. (BAE SYSTEMS Heritage)

The Blind Landing Experimental Unit operated this One-Eleven, which displays the military serial XX105. The aircraft had been acquired from British Caledonian Airways and subsequently served with the Defence Research Agency and QinetiQ until 2003. (BAE SYSTEMS Heritage)

others in 1962 as a replacement for the de Havilland Heron but passed over in favour of the Hawker Siddeley Andover, a move which involved little capital expenditure since the turboprops had already been ordered for the RAF.

The One-Eleven was again under consideration in 1979. A specification for a Queen's Flight variant had been drawn up in 1971 and was reconsidered in 1977. By 1979, the concept was changed from a short-to-medium-range aircraft with modifications to increase its range to 2,400 miles. In April 1980, Prince Philip made a series of flights from Benson in BAC's development aircraft G-ASYD. It had been planned that the last two Series 475 One-Elevens off the UK production line would have been used by the Queen's Flight to fly members of Royal Household on official business around the world. But, in 1984, it was announced that, after a detailed evaluation, the BAe 146 had been chosen instead.

Northrop-Grumman's two ex-American Airlines' Series 400s were given civilian registrations, although they have been used for military research. They have served as test beds for programmes like the B-1B bomber and F-16 fighter as well as testing radar and avionics installations on the F-22 and YF-23. One of the aircraft was converted by Lockheed-Martin to test avionics for the Joint Strike Fighter.

Military One-Eleven variants not proceeded with included an airborne early warning aircraft with 24ft diameter fuselage-mounted radome, a maritime patrol aircraft for the Japanese Maritime Air Self-Defence Force with a new wing, Series 400 fuselage, additional under-wing engines and weapons bay, and a casualty evacuation aircraft for the US Air Force Military Airlift Command.

Chapter 9
What Might Have Been

B y the late 1970s, the Labour government was preparing to put into effect its long-cherished plan to nationalise the nation's aircraft industry with the creation of one company, British Aerospace. At the same time, the government was supporting the development of the 146 four-engined regional airliner, a programme that had the strong support of the new company's trade unions. The 146 was originally a Hawker Siddeley project.

But in 1982, BAe became aware of interest from some operators in re-engining suitable One-Eleven airframes. The engine proposed was the Rolls-Royce Tay, which offered 15,000lb of thrust. It also promised better range and lower maintenance costs. The Tay was also less noisy than the Spey: as more stringent noise regulations were in prospect, this was a matter of concern to operators faced with hush-kitting costs of around £1m per aircraft.

Tay One-Eleven

In 1983, BAe formally offered the Tay engine to One-Eleven operators at US$5.5m per aircraft. This was based on adapting 35. But the expected support from major UK operators like BA and BCal failed to materialise, and BAe withdrew the programme.

But, in the US, Dee Howard of the Dee Howard Corporation of San Antonio, Texas, decided to go ahead with his own project. He quickly discovered that there were few major technical difficulties involved and considered there was a good case for offering conversions for the Series 500 One-Eleven, which promised a performance superior to the 146-300.

The programme was launched in January 1986 with the promise of a first flight in mid-1987, but it was not until July 1990 that the Tay-powered One-Eleven took to the air. The aircraft was demonstrated at that year's Farnborough Airshow. A second flew in 1991, but the programme failed because it had taken too long to progress and through lack of support, even though the Romanians had shown interest in it.

Series 670

A plan to offer a Series 475 derivative, known the Series 670, as a replacement for the indigenous NAMC YS-11 turboprop to Japanese carriers resulted in the BAC development aircraft, G-ASYD, appearing in yet another guise in September 1977. But hopes of a significant sales break-through, in what had hitherto been a closed market for the One-Eleven, were to be frustrated. Despite major improvements in performance, the Series 670 was rejected due to stringent regulatory requirements.

Series 600

There were several One-Eleven developments that did not progress beyond the drawing board. The Series 600 was a proposed Series 500 development with an extended fuselage and increased wing area. A key feature was to have been developed Spey Mk 512-14DW engines having an aft fan immediately behind the engine thrust reverse unit. This would have involved the realignment of the engine mountings as well as some redesign of the nacelle and the stub fairings on which they were mounted. The water injection system would have been retained and power was expected to rise to 19,370lb of thrust.

The fuselage would have been extended with the insertion of two plugs, one of 13ft 4in forward of the wing and the other 2ft 2in aft. The rear over-wing emergency exits were deleted while the forward one was moved forward 1ft 11.5in. Further emergency exits were added between the wing and the

Is this how the One-Eleven should have been developed? Sir George Edwards believed the One-Eleven might have rivalled the success of the DC-9 and Boeing 737 had it been equipped with Pratt & Whitney JT8D engines. This British Aerospace artist's impression shows it was more than just a pipe dream, but Edwards was well aware that putting an American engine in a British aircraft would raise objections. (BAE SYSTEMS Heritage)

engines with the starboard door also acting as a service door. Bigger wheels and tyres meant moving the main undercarriage bay aft bulkhead rearwards to accommodate them. An additional cargo door, forward of the wing, was specified. A 17 per cent increase in wing area was achieved by lengthening the wingspan by 5ft with an extended centre section. There would have been a new flap section, but the Series 500 wingtip extension was deleted. Both tailplane and fin area were increased, and the tail bullet deleted.

The forward passenger entry door and airstairs, together with the rear ventral airstairs, were retained with a third toilet added immediately aft of the forward entry door. Various cabin layouts were proposed including a high capacity one with 136 seats at 29/32in pitch. This variant was announced in September 1968, and first deliveries would have been offered by 1972.

A considerably less radical version was proposed to BA in January 1978. It would have retained the standard Series 500 fuselage, fin and tailplane with a wing incorporating the leading edge adopted for late production Series 500s. Revised flap settings would have improved airfield performance. Improved Spey Mk.514-14 engines using RB211 technology were expected to give increased power, greater combustion efficiency and a 60 per cent reduction in noise. An optional 350-gallon fuel tank in the hold area would have given the aircraft an extra 200 nautical miles range with maximum payload, although hold capacity was reduced. A reworked interior was also proposed.

Series 700

The Series 700 was a further Series 500 development, which was announced in November 1973. This variant would have been powered by the Rolls-Royce RB163-67B, later named Spey Mk 606. It offered 16,900lb of thrust through a development of the Spey 512 in which the five-stage low-pressure compressor was replaced by a single stage fan and a three-stage compressor on the same shaft. A third low-pressure turbine stage would have been added. The existing 12 stage Mk 512 high pressure system would have been retained but with advanced turbine cooling technology. The engine was expected to meet present and expected noise requirements even when operated at maximum take-off weights. Fuel consumption would have been considerably improved.

This proposed aircraft featured an extended fuselage with two plugs, a forward one of 8ft 4in and a rear one of 3ft 8in. Emergency exits were similar to those proposed for the Series 600, but the ventral entrance was now optional. There was a new rear door between the wing and the engines. Once again, the original forward doors and airstairs would have been retained. This variant had the standard Series 500 wing, but it was strengthened to cope with increased weights and there were minor changes to flaps, flap carriages and tracks.

In February 1978, the Weybridge Project Office announced a development of the Series 700 powered by Rolls-Royce RB.432 engines. Other changes over the Series 700 included increased area for the fin and rudder. This variant was not allocated a new series number but could have been in service by 1977.

Series 800

The final One-Eleven variant was announced in March 1975. The Series 800 proposed an even bigger fuselage stretch and use of 22,000lb thrust CFM56 turbofans. There would have been a forward fuselage plug 24ft 2in long with a rearward one of 8ft 4in. A cabin seating up to 161 passengers at 30in pitch or 144 at 33/34in was offered. Three galleys and three toilets were planned, and the increased seating would have called for eight emergency exits. The tailplane and fin would both have been extended with a bigger wing.

This display model indicates how the BAC One-Eleven Series 800 might have appeared. With its extended fuselage capable of seating up to 161 passengers and pair of CFM56 turbofan engines, it certainly stretched the original One-Eleven concept. (BAE SYSTEMS Heritage)

More radical proposals had emerged from BAC in the 1960s, which in hindsight represented the industry's last chance to remain an independent manufacturer of major civil aircraft. But these ideas came at a time of great uncertainty about the advisability of joining a European consortium that eventually became Airbus. In the end, Britain missed out on the BAC Two-Eleven and the wide-bodied Three-Eleven, and the government declined to join the Airbus project.

The Two-Eleven

The Two-Eleven was essentially a scaled-up One-Eleven with a pair of rear-mounted Rolls-Royce RB211 high by-pass ratio turbofans each offering 36,000lb of thrust. Seating for up to 219 passengers in a high density six-abreast layout or a two-class configuration for 176 was proposed. The wing and tail would have been scaled up from the One-Eleven, and the Two-Eleven was expected to offer a range of 1,380 nautical miles at maximum payload. BAC thought the aircraft could make its first flight in 1970 and be in service with BEA by 1972. Airframe development costs were put at £60m. BEA was enthusiastic, and Laker Airways and Autair liked it so much they ordered three and two examples, respectively, but the government announced in December 1967 that it would not be supporting the project.

The Three-Eleven

The Three-Eleven took the One-Eleven format to its logical conclusion although it owed little to the smaller aircraft beyond its rear-mounted engines and T-tail. Announced in 1968, with RB211 power and seating for up to 300 passengers in a nine-abreast configuration, it was the biggest airliner planned by a British manufacturer. At the time of its announcement, the government was backing the Airbus A300 and its response was lukewarm. Once it had disengaged from Airbus, it become more enthusiastic, but a change of administration meant more delay as the incoming Conservative government had to consider whether or not it would support the project.

The airlines also liked the Three-Eleven. Laker Airways wanted it and BEA placed a provisional contract at the 1970 Farnborough Airshow. Although the promising Three-Eleven would have represented Britain's entry ticket to the wide-bodied club, the project was brought down by its engines. The advanced technology of the RB211 proved to be beyond Rolls-Royce, and the company's efforts to develop the engine pushed it into insolvency and nationalisation. The result was that there was no cash left to support the Three-Eleven and so the project died.

Between 1963 and 1984, 235 examples of the BAC One-Eleven were built in the UK, all but 13 of them at Hurn. Nine more were assembled in Romania to produce a grand total of 244. Half a century

Seating in the Three-Eleven could have been arranged in six, eight or nine abreast. This mock-up features a nine-abreast seating configuration.

Mock-up of the Three-Eleven's flight deck.

Last of the line. The Three-Eleven was the ultimate projected One-Eleven development with a wide-body and Rolls-Royce RB211 turbo-fan engines. Offering seating for up to 300 passengers in a nine-abreast configuration, the Three-Eleven would have been the biggest airliner planned by a British manufacturer – had it been built.

ago, its future had seemed assured judging by the level of support received even before the prototype had completed its maiden flight. By contrast the DC-9, its only real competitor at the time, appeared to be lagging behind. Yet a total of 976 DC-9s have been built, plus 1,191 MD-80s.

It could be argued that the failure to fully capitalise on the One-Eleven's initial success was one of the major lost opportunities in British airliner history. So, could a developed version have dominated the world market for regional airliners? Sir George Edwards' answer in 2006 was unequivocal: 'without a shadow of doubt when you think of all the DC-9s that were built after we canned the One-Eleven'.

The fact is that a lack of suitable engine limited the One-Eleven's chances. Once the Rolls-Royce Medway had been cancelled, there was nothing available for a stretched One-Eleven although there was talk of using the Pratt & Whitney JT8D. Edwards' biographer notes, however, that he was well aware that 'such a move was full of risk both technically and financially especially as it would probably require designing a new beefed-up wing. And by then new alternative projects were in the offing, such as the projected larger BAC Two-Eleven'.

Later came more politics and the Hawker Siddeley 146. At one stage, the four-engined regional jet had been rejected as a candidate for launch aid, but in the late 1970s, strong trade union support encouraged the government to favour it over a developed One-Eleven. By the time of BAe Systems' decision to end decades of complete civil airliner manufacturer in the UK, 387 BAe 146s and Avro RJs had been produced.

Accidents and Incidents

'Mayday, Mayday, Mayday – London, this is Speedbird Five Three Nine Zero. Mayday, Mayday, Mayday'. The controller acknowledged: 'Speedbird Five Three Nine Zero. Roger, Mayday acknowledged. Out'.

A few seconds later: 'Speedbird Five Three Nine Zero. Emergency depressurisation on a radar heading of one nine five. Descending to flight level one hundred [10,000ft]'.

It signalled the start of an hour-long drama that had begun as the cabin crew of BA Flight 5390 travelling from Birmingham to Malaga on 10 June 1990 were about to serve the 81 passengers their breakfast. BAC One-Eleven Series 528 G-BJRT *City of Glamorgan* was commanded by Captain Tim Lancaster.

Suddenly, there was a loud bang. The cabin quickly filled with condensation. On the flight deck, the pilot's windscreen blew out. Lancaster was sucked from his seat and halfway through the roaring gap. His upper torso was outside the aircraft leaving only his legs inside. The flight deck door had blown inwards and was now blocking the throttle controls. Papers and other debris were blowing about. The aircraft was diving and speed was building up.

Flight attendant Nigel Ogden was on the flight deck at the time. He grabbed Lancaster's belt with both hands as the captain's torso was being blasted by the 500mph airstream. Inside the cabin, the two stewardesses began reassuring the passengers and securing loose objects.

First Officer Alastair Atchison, an experienced pilot with 1,000 hours on the One-Eleven, had to descend to denser air while trying to establish control and handle the radio. The noise made it difficult for him to hear the messages from LATCC.

Ogden was still clutching Lancaster although the captain had shifted a little further out of the cockpit. But the steward was beginning to suffer from frostbite and losing his strength. Lancaster's face kept hitting the cockpit window. The crew did not know if he was alive or dead, but Atchison insisted they must not let go.

Six minutes went by before he made LATCC understand the full extent of his predicament. There was also a delay in BA being informed. Atchison was then given a choice of an emergency landing at Gatwick or Southampton. He requested radar assistance to Southampton.

At 0744hrs, Southampton Tower contacted Atchison. The One-Eleven was now six miles west of the airport and leaving flight level six-four (6,400ft). Thirty seconds later, Atchison radioed that he was unfamiliar with the airport. He added: 'I request you shepherd me on to the runway, please'. Asked for the number on board he replied: 'We have 84 persons, sir and I think that will be all until we're on the ground'.

A minute later, Atchison requested emergency facilities for the captain. 'I think he's dead,' he added. The One-Eleven was cleared to make an emergency landing. It was down at 0755hrs. Passengers immediately disembarked from the front and rear stairs. Emergency crews recovered Lancaster and took him to hospital. He was certainly not dead but suffering from frostbite, bruising and shock. His right arm, left thumb and right wrist were fractured. Flight attendant Nigel Ogden sustained a dislocated shoulder and frostbite. Lancaster was back at work less than five months later and retired from British Airways when he reached the age of 55. No one else suffered any injuries.

The One-Eleven's windscreen was found on the ground in Oxfordshire. Still attached to it were 11 of the bolts used to fasten it to the aircraft. Another 18 were found loose. Accident investigators determined that of the 90 fasteners 84 were the wrong ones. The screen had been changed by the BA engineering night shift at Birmingham airport on the night of 8/9 June.

In its report of the incident, the Air Accidents Investigation Branch noted: 'The crew were faced with an instantaneous and unforeseen emergency. The combined actions of the co-pilot and cabin crew successfully avoided what could have been a major catastrophe. The fact that all those on board the aircraft survived is a tribute to their quick thinking and perseverance in the face of a shocking experience'. Atchison and flight attendant Susan Gibbins were awarded the Queen's Commendation for Valuable Service in the Air.

The drama of BA 5390 was one of the more bizarre incidents in the One-Eleven's long service life. Not all ended well: there were fatalities in 14 accidents involving One-Elevens. Including the first prototype, two were lost before the type went into commercial service. But the first accidents involving passengers came in 1966, when a Braniff Airways Series 200 flying between Kansas City and Omaha exploded in mid-air near Falls City, Nebraska, with 42 killed. The aircraft was seen to enter cloud shortly before the accident.

A year later, a Mohawk Airlines aircraft crashed near Blossburg, Pennsylvania, with the loss of 34 lives. The accident was attributed to an in-flight fire that broke out in the rear fuselage near the auxiliary power unit. All aircraft in service at the time were examined and corrective action taken to non-return air valves.

According to the Flight Safety Foundation's Aviation Safety Database, the worst BAC One-Eleven accident in terms of the number of lives lost was recorded at the end of the type's service career. In May 2002, an aircraft of Nigerian airline EAS Airlines crashed at Kano with the loss of 149 lives including 78 killed on the ground.

Altogether, the database lists 31 accidents involving the loss of One-Eleven hulls:

A total of 31 BAC One-Eleven hulls were lost in accidents, but none of those operated by British Airways and its predecessor BEA were among them. However, British Airways' G-BJRT was the subject of a bizarre incident on Sunday 10 June 1990 when part of its windscreen suddenly popped out at altitude. The captain was sucked from the flight deck but survived the incident as the first officer was able to make an emergency landing. Pictured here is a sister ship. (Tom Singfield)

Date	Type	Registration	Operator	Location	Fatalities
22 Oct 1963	200AB	G-ASHG	BAC	Near Cricklade	7
18 Mar 1964	200AC	G-ASJB	BAC	Wisley	-
06 Aug 1966	203AE	N1553	Braniff	Falls City, NE	42
23 Jun 1967	204AF	N1116J	Mohawk	Blossburg, PA	34
14 Jan 1969	201AC	GASJJ	BUA	Milan-Linate	-
12 Sept 1967	402AP	PI-C1131	Philippine Air Lines	Manila Intl.	45
07 Dec 1970	424EU	YR-BCA	Tarom	Constanta	19
06 Sept 1971	515FH	D-ALAR	Paninternational	Hamburg	22
04 Dec 1973	521FH	LV-JNR	Austral Linea Aereas	Bahia Blanca	-
01 Feb 1974	520FN	PP-SDQ	Transbrasil	Sao Paulo	-
09 Feb 1975	401AK	N711ST	Jet Travel	Lake Tahoe airport, CA	-
23 May 1976	527FK	RP-C1161	Philippine Air Lines	Zamboanga	13
04 Jan 1977	520N	PP-SDS	Transbrasil	Sao Paulo	-
21 Nov 1977	420EL	LV-JGY	Austral Lineas Aereas	San Carlos de Bariloche, Argentina	46
09 Jul 1978	203AE	N1550	Allegheny	Rochester, NY	-
07 May 1981	529FR	LV-LOX	Austral Lineas Aereas	Buenos Aires	31
04 Aug 1984	527FK	RP-C1182	Philippine Air Lines	Tacloban	-
21 Jul 1989	516FP	RP-C1193	Philippine Air Lines	Manila Intl.	8 on ground
07 Sept 1989	320AZ	5N-AOT	Okada Air	Port Harcourt	-
26 Jun 1991	402AP	5N-AOW	Okada Air	Sokoto airport	3
16 Sept 1991	204AF	5N-KBG	Kabo Air	Port Harcourt	-
23 Aug 1992	204AF	5N-KBA	Kabo Air	Sokoto airport	-
29 Aug 1992	208AL	5N-HTA	Hold Trade Air	Kaduna airport	-
18 Sept 1994	515FB	5N-IMO	Oriental Airlines	Tamanrasset Aguiemar airport, Algeria	5
30 Dec 1995	525FT	YR-BCO	Tarom	Istanbul	-
07 Jun 1997	525FT	YR-BCM	Tarom	Stockholm	-
29 Jul 1997	203AE	5N-BAA	ADC Airlines	Calabar airport	1
28 Aug 2001	412EB	5N-BDC	Eagle Aviation	Libreville, Gabon	-
27 Mar 2002	401AK	5N-MBM	Albarka Air	Abuja	-
27 Mar 2002	523FJ	5N-BDU	Savannah Airlines	Abuja	-
04 May 2002	525FT	5N-ESF	EAS Airlines	Kano	71 plus 78 on ground

Specifications and Variants

BAC ONE-ELEVEN SERIES 200

Flight crew	2
Seating capacity	89
Length	93ft 6in (28.50m)
Height	24ft 6in (7.47m)
Wingspan	88ft 6in (26.98m)
Wing area	980sq ft (91.04sq m)
Empty weight	46,405lb (21,049kg)
Max take-off weight	79,000lb (35,833kg)
Max cruise speed	548mph (882km/h)
Still air range with max fuel	2,130 miles (3,430km)
Powerplant	two Rolls-Royce Spey 506-14 turbofans each generating 10,410lb (46.3kN) thrust

BAC ONE-ELEVEN VARIANTS SUMMARY

Series 200: initial production variant; 58 built

Series 300: Spey Mk 511 engines each developing 10,410lb (51 kN) thrust plus additional fuel capacity to increase range; nine built

Series 400: Series 300 with US instrumentation and equipment; 70 built

Series 475: Series 400 body and Series 500 wing with 5ft (1.52m) longer span and powerplant and equipped for operation from unpaved runways; 13 built

Series 500: 13ft 6in (4.12m) longer body with seating for up to 119 passengers, 5ft (1.52m) longer wingspan and Spey Mk 512s each producing 12,550 lb (55.8 kN) thrust; 87 completed; British European Airways' Series 510EDs (Super One-Elevens) had Smiths Industries avionics to provide commonality with Hawker Siddeley Trident but this variant required a specific type-rating for crews

Rombac Series 560: Romanian-built Series 500; nine built

Series 670: Series 475 derivative with improved aerodynamics and hush-kitted engines; one converted

BAC One-Eleven Production List

Construction number	Series	Initial	First operator registration	Date of first flight	Date of delivery
004	200AB	G-ASHG	BAC	20 Aug 1963	-
005	201AC	G-ASJA	BUA	19 Dec 1963	11 Oct 1965
006	201AC	G-ASJB	BUA	14 Feb 1964	-
007	201AC	G-ASJC	BUA	01 Apr 1964	06 Nov 1965
008	201AC	G-ASJD	BUA	06 Jul 1964	05 Aug 1965
009	201AC	G-ASJE	BUA	05 May 1964	23 Jul 1965
010	201AC	G-ASJF	BUA	28 Jul 1964	22 May 1965
011	201AC	G-ASJG	BUA	31 Oct 1964	06 Jul 1965
012	201AC	G-ASJH	BUA	17 Sept 1964	17 Apr 1965
013	201AC	G-ASJI	BUA	22 Dec 1964	15 Apr 1965
014	201AC	G-ASJJ	BUA	24 Feb 1965	06 Apr 1965
015	203AE	N1541	Braniff	09 Jun 1964	10 Aug 1965
016	203AE	N1542	Braniff	30 Oct 1964	20 Apr 1965
017	203AE	N1543	Braniff	10 Feb 1965	11 Mar 1965
018	203AE	N1544	Braniff	26 Mar 1965	06 Apr 1965
019	203AE	N1545	Braniff	10 May 1965	12 May 1965
020	203AE	N1546	Braniff	30 May 1965	02 Jun 1965
029	204AF	N2111J	Mohawk	04 May 1965	15 May 1965
030	204AF	N1112J	Mohawk	19 Jun 1965	25 Jun 1965
031	204AF	N1113J	Mohawk	03 Aug 1965	10 Aug 1965
032	204AF	N1114J	Mohawk	26 Sept 1965	29 Sept 1965
033	301AG	G-ATPJ	British Eagle	20 May 1966	08 Jun 1966
034	301AG	G-ATPK	British Eagle	14 Jun 1966	24 Jun 1966
035	301AG	G-ATPL	British Eagle	13 Jul 1966	22 Jul 1966
039	207AJ	G-ATTP	British Eagle	19 Feb 1966	22 Apr 1966
040	207AJ	G-ATVH	British Eagle	16 Apr 1966	21 May 1966
041	203AE	N1547	Braniff	18 Jul 1965	20 Jul 1965
042	203AE	N1548	Braniff	15 Aug 1965	18 Aug 1965

Construction number	Series	Initial	First operator registration	Date of first flight	Date of delivery
043	203AE	N1549	Braniff	20 Sept 1965	24 Sept 1965
044	203AE	N1550	Braniff	01 Oct 1965	04 Oct 1965
045	203AE	N1551	Braniff	03 Nov 1965	08 Nov 1965
046	203AE	N1552	Braniff	22 Nov 1965	24 Nov 1965
049	208AL	EI-ANE	Aer Lingus	28 Apr 1965	14 May 1965
050	208AL	EI-ANF	Aer Lingus	09 Jun 1965	12 Jun 1965
051	208AL	EI-ANG	Aer Lingus	24 Jul 1965	31 Jul 1965
052	208AL	EI-ANH	Aer Lingus	27 Aug 1965	09 Sept 1965
053	400AM	G-ASYD	BAC	13 Jul 1965	n/a
054	410AQ	N3939V	Victor Comptometers Inc	16 Sept 1965	08 Sept 1966
055	401AK	N5015	American Airlines	04 Nov 1965	23 Dec 1965
056	401AK	N5016	American Airlines	08 Dec 1965	22 Jan 1966
057	401AK	N5017	American Airlines	03 Jan 1966	29 Jan 1966
058	401AK	N5018	American Airlines	15 Jan 1966	15 Feb 1966
059	401AK	N5019	American Airlines	29 Jan 1966	24 Feb 1966
060	401AK	N5020	American Airlines	06 Feb 1966	13 Mar 1966
061	401AK	N5021	American Airlines	16 Feb 1966	04 Mar 1966
062	401AK	N5022	American Airlines	03 Mar 1966	17 Mar 1966
063	401AK	N5023	American Airlines	05 Mar 1966	21 Mar 1966
064	401AK	N5024	American Airlines	24 Mar 1966	15 Apr 1966
065	401AK	N5025	American Airlines	25 Mar 1966	07 Apr 1966
066	401AK	N5026	American Airlines	08 Apr 1966	23 Apr 1966
067	401AK	N5027	American Airlines	16 Apr 1966	29 Apr 1966
068	401AK	N5028	American Airlines	26 Apr 1966	10 May 1966
069	401AK	N5029	American Airlines	03 May 1966	21 May 1966
070	203AE	N1553	Braniff	05 Dec 1965	08 Dec 1965
071	203AE	N1554	Braniff	19 Dec 1965	22 Dec 1965
072	401AK	N5030	American Airlines	12 May 1966	27 May 1966
073	401AK	N5031	American Airlines	21 May 1966	09 Jun 1966
074	401AK	N5032	American Airlines	06 June 1966	21 Jun 1966
075	401AK	N5033	American Airlines	10 Jun 1966	27 Jun 1966
076	401AK	N5034	American Airlines	25 Jun 1966	09 Jul 1966
077	401AK	N5035	American Airlines	01 Jul 1966	22 Jul 1966
078	401AK	N5036	American Airlines	23 Jul 1966	04 Aug 1966

Construction number	Series	Initial	First operator registration	Date of first flight	Date of delivery
079	401AK	N5037	American Airlines	06 Aug 1966	19 Aug 1966
080	401AK	N5038	American Airlines	23 Aug 1966	08 Sept 1966
081	401AK	N5039	American Airlines	01 Oct 1966	12 Oct 1966
082	204AF	N1115J	Mohawk	19 Nov 1965	21 Nov 1965
083	212AR	N502T	Tenneco	02 Mar 1966	05 Apr 1966
084	211AH	D-ABHH	Horten	15 Jan 1966	29 Jan 1966
085	201AC	G-ASTJ	BUA	25 Oct 1965	09 Nov 1965
086	401AK	N5040	American Airlines	14 Oct 1966	28 Oct 1966
087	401AK	N5041	American Airlines	29 Oct 1966	10 Nov 1966
088	401AK	N5042	American Airlines	09 Nov 1966	19 Nov 1966
089	401AK	N5043	American Airlines	21 Nov 1966	10 Dec 1966
090	401AK	N5044	American Airlines	06 Dec 1966	16 Dec 1966
091	402AP	PI-C1121	Philippine Airlines	07 Apr 1966	19 Apr 1966
092	402AP	PI-C1131	Philippine Airlines	17 Sept 1966	24 Sept 1966
093	407AW	YS-17C	TACA	05 Dec 1966	14 Dec 1966
094	402AP	G-AVEJ	Bavaria Flug	03 Jan 1967	23 Mar 1967
096	215AU	N11181	Aloha Airlines	06 Apr 1966	15 Apr 1966
097	215AU	N11182	Aloha Airlines	30 May 1966	07 Jun 1966
098	204AF	N1116J	Mohawk	01 Aug 1966	05 Aug 1966
099	204AF	N1117J	Mohawk	26 Aug 1966	30 Aug 1966
100	204AF	N1118J	Mohawk	20 Sept 1966	26 Sept 1966
101	204AF	N1119J	Mohawk	11 Oct 1966	15 Oct 1966
102	204AF	N1120J	Mohawk	06 Jan 1967	24 Jan 1967
103	204AF	N1122J	Mohawk	10 Aug 1967	17 Aug 1967
104	204AF	N1123J	Mohawk	19 Dec 1967	30 Dec 1967
105	215AU	N11183	Aloha Airlines	26 May 1967	31 May 1967
106	407AW	YS-18C	TACA	03 Feb 1967	21 Feb 1967
107	320AZ	G-AVBW	Laker Airways	17 Feb 1967	25 Feb 1967
108	409AY	TI-1056C	LACSA	06 Mar 1967	14 Apr 1967
109	320AZ	G-AVBX	Laker Airways	28 Mar 1967	08 Apr 1967
110	304AX	G-ATPH	British Eagle	19 Apr 1967	28 Apr 1967
111	412EB	AN-BBI	LANICA	08 Apr 1967	20 Apr 1967
112	304AX	G-ATPI	British Eagle	12 May 1967	25 May 1967
113	320AZ	G-AVBY	Laker Airways	01 May 1967	09 May 1967
114	408EF	G-AVGP	Channel Airways	09 Jun 1967	14 Jun 1967
115	408EF	G-AWEJ	Channel Airways	01 May 1968	10 May 1968

Construction number	Series	Initial	First operator registration	Date of first flight	Date of delivery
116	413FA	G-AWGG	Bavaria Flug	20 Jun 1968	25 Jun 1968
117	420EL	LV-JGX	ALA	10 Aug 1968	25 Sept 1968
118	423ET	VC-92-2111	Forca Aerea Brasileira	12 Oct 1967	15 Oct 1968
119	422EQ	PP-SRT	VASP	18 Oct 1967	19 Dec 1967
120	419EP	N270E	Englehard Industries	08 Aug 1967	21 Sept 1967
121	432FD	VP-BCY	Bahamas Airways	28 Aug 1968	11 Nov 1968
122	420EL	LV-IZR	Austral	21 Jul 1967	12 Oct 1967
123	420EL	LV-IZS	Austral	05 Sept 1967	08 Nov 1967
124	217EA	A12-124	Royal Australian Air Force	03 Nov 1967	12 Jan 1968
125	217EA	A12-125	Royal Australian Air Force	10 Jan 1968	31 Jan 1968
126	422EQ	PP-SRU	VASP	08 Nov 1967	19 Dec 1967
127	414EG	D-ANDY	Bavaria Flug	06 Dec 1967	29 Dec 1967
128	408EF	G-AWKJ	Channel Airways	29 Jan 1969	31 Mar 1969
129	416EK	G-AVOE	Autair	08 Mar 1968	19 Mar 1968
130	424EU	YR-BCA	TAROM	23 Jan 1968	14 Jun 1968
131	416EK	G-AVOF	Autair	18 Jan 1968	08 Feb 1968
132	416EK	G-AWBL	Autair	22 Apr 1968	01 May 1968
133	320AZ	G-AVYZ	Laker Airways	08 Apr 1968	11 Apr 1968
134	204AF	N1124J	Mohawk	04 Mar 1968	25 Mar 1968
135	204AF	N1125J	Mohawk	11 Jun 1968	17 Jun 1968
136	510ED	G-AVMH	BEA	07 Feb 1968	12 Jun 1969
137	510ED	G-AVMI	BEA	13 May 1968	02 Apr 1969
138	510ED	G-AVMJ	BEA	15 Jul 1968	29 Aug 1968
139	510ED	G-AVMK	BEA	08 Aug 1968	16 Sept 1968
140	510ED	G-AVML	BEA	30 Aug 1968	04 Oct 1968
141	510ED	G-AVMM	BEA	28 Sept 1968	25 Oct 1968
142	510ED	G-AVMN	BEA	14 Oct 1968	20 Nov 1968
143	510ED	G-AVMO	BEA	29 Oct 1968	27 Nov 1968
144	510ED	G-AVMP	BEA	05 Nov 1968	11 Dec 1968
145	510ED	G-AVMR	BEA	28 Nov 1968	05 May 1970
146	510ED	G-AVMS	BEA	14 Dec 1968	13 Jan 1969
147	510ED	G-AVMT	BEA	10 Jan 1969	28 Mar 1969

Construction number	Series	Initial	First operator registration	Date of first flight	Date of delivery
148	510ED	G-AVMU	BEA	29 Jan 1969	19 Mar 1969
149	510ED	G-AVMV	BEA	21 Mar 1969	21 Apr 1969
150	510ED	G-AVMW	BEA	27 Apr 1969	02 May 1969
151	510ED	G-AVMX	BEA	02 Jun 1969	20 Jun 1969
152	510ED	G-AVMY	BEA	09 Jul 1969	21 Jul 1969
153	510ED	G-AVMZ	BEA	05 Aug 1969	15 Aug 1969
154	423ET	VC-92-2110	FAB	09 Oct 1968	13 May 1969
155	420EL	LV-JGY	Austral	08 Nov 1968	17 Dec 1968
156	424EU	YR-BCB	Tarom	11 Dec 1968	17 Dec 1968
157	432FD	VP-BCZ	Bahamas Airways	27 Nov 1968	04 Dec 1968
158	414EG	D-AISY	Bavaria Flug	17 Apr 1970	22 Apr 1970
159	424EU	YR-BCD	TAROM	22 Jul 1969	30 Jul 1969
160	414EG	D-ANNO	Bavaria Flug	19 Dec 1970	22 Dec 1970
161	402AP	EC-BQF	TAE	20 Sept 1968	15 Mar 1969
162	409AY	TI-1055C	LACSA	14 Feb 1969	05 Nov 1969
163	414EG	D-AILY	Bavaria Flug	26 Jan 1970	26 Feb 1970
165	424EU	YR-BCE	Tarom	29 Sept 1969	23 Nov 1969
166	416EK	G-AWXJ	Autair	27 Feb 1969	20 Mar 1969
167	424EU	YR-BCC	Tarom	26 Jun 1969	03 Jul 1969
168	424EU	YR-BCF	Tarom	18 Nov 1969	13 Dec 1969
174	501EX	G-AWYR	BUA	25 Mar 1969	11 Apr 1969
175	501EX	G-AWYS	BUA	16 Apr 1969	24 Apr 1969
176	501EX	G-AWYT	BUA	06 May 1969	13 May 1969
177	501EX	G-AWYU	BUA	10 Jun 1969	17 Jun 1969
178	501EX	G-AWYV	BUA	20 Jun 1969	26 Jun 1969
179	204AF	N1126J	Mohawk	15 Jul 1968	02 Aug 1968
180	204AF	N1127J	Mohawk	10 Dec 1968	31 Dec 1968
181	204AF	N1128J	Mohawk	10 Jan 1969	21 Jan 1969
182	204AF	N1129J	Mohawk	12 May 1969	17 May 1969
183	212AR	N503T	Tenneco	07 Jun 1969	08 Jul 1969
184	509EW	G-AWWX	Caledonian Airways	11 Feb 1969	29 Mar 1969
185	509EW	G-AWWY	Caledonian Airways	11 Mar 1969	31 Mar 1969
186	509EW	G-AWWZ	Caledonian Airways	18 Apr 1969	28 Apr 1969

Construction number	Series	Initial	First operator registration	Date of first flight	Date of delivery
187	515FB	D-ALAT	Panair International	22 May 1969	13 Jun 1969
188	517FE	VP-BCN	Bahamas Airways	17 Jul 1969	23 Jul 1969
189	517FE	VP-BCO	Bahamas Airways	21 Jul 1969	29 Jul 1969
190	524FF	D-AMIE	Germanair	02 Sept 1969	17 Oct 1969
191	501EX	G-AXJK	BUA	14 Aug 1969	05 Mar 1970
192	521FH	LV-JNR	Austral	15 Sept 1969	21 Nov 1969
193	523FJ	G-AXLL	British Midland Airways	25 Sept 1969	17 Feb 1970
194	521FH	LV-JNS	Austral	08 Oct 1969	18 Nov 1969
195	524FF	D-AMUR	Germanair	20 Oct 1969	16 Dec 1969
196	521FH	LV-JNT	ALA	06 Nov 1969	25 Nov 1969
197	524FF	D-AMOR	Germanair	09 Dec 1969	20 Mar 1970
198	517FE	VP-LAN	LIAT/Court Line	12 Jan 1970	20 Jun 1972
199	523FJ	G-AXLM	British Midland Airways	26 Dec 1969	05 Mar 1970
200	518FG	G-AXMF	Court Line	25 Nov 1969	05 Dec 1969
201	518FG	G-AXMG	Court Line	08 Dec 1969	18 Dec 1969
202	518FG	G-AXMH	Court Line	12 Jan 1970	11 Feb 1970
203	518FG	G-AXMI	Court Line	27 Jan 1970	24 Mar 1970
204	518FG	G-AXMJ	Court Line	17 Feb 1970	12 Mar 1970
205	518FG	G-AXMK	Court Line	07 Mar 1970	21 Apr 1970
206	518FG	G-AXML	Court Line	22 Apr 1970	30 Apr 1970
207	515FB	D-ALAR	Paninternational	01 May 1970	13 May 1970
208	515FB	D-ALAS	Paninternational	13 Mar 1970	20 Mar 1970
209	501EX	G-AXJL	BUA	20 Feb 1970	05 Mar 1970
210	509EW	G-AXYD	Caledonian Airways	06 Mar 1970	18 Mar 1970
211	523FJ	G-AXLN	British Midland Airways	04 Feb 1970	12 Mar 1970
212	529AR	HB-ITL	Phoenix Airways	14 May 1970	01 Apr 1971
213	527FK	PI-C1161	Philippine Airlines	15 Sept 1970	26 Oct 1971
214	501EX	G-AXJM	BUA	17 Mar 1970	25 Mar 1970
215	527FK	PI-C1171	Philippine Airlines	09 Oct 1970	29 Oct 1971
226	527FK	PI-C1181	Philippine Airlines	03 Nov 1970	05 Nov 1971
227	528FL	D-AMUC	Bavaria Flug	28 Oct 1970	03 Dec 1970

Construction number	Series	Initial	First operator registration	Date of first flight	Date of delivery
228	520FN	PP-SDQ	Sadia	21 Sept 1970	15 Oct 1970
229	515FB	D-ALAQ	Paninternational	04 Dec 1970	04 Mar 1971
230	520FN	PP-SDR	Sadia	11 Nov 1970	31 Dec 1970
231	516FP	TG-AZA	Aviateca	16 Dec 1970	25 Mar 1971
232	518FG	G-AYOR	Court Line	29 Jan 1971	18 Mar 1971
233	518FG	G-AYOP	Court Line	03 Mar 1971	31 Mar 1971
234	528FL	D-ALFA	Bavaria Flug	08 Feb 1971	26 Feb 1971
235	524FF	D-AMAT	Germanair	17 Apr 1971	08 May 1971
236	520FN	PP-SDS	Transbrasil	30 Apr 1971	23 Sept 1972
237	531FS	TI-1084C	LACSA	13 May 1971	26 May 1971
238	528FL	D-ANUE	Bavaria Flug	28 Feb 1972	15 Mar 1972
239	476FM	OB-R-953	Faucett Airways	05 Apr 1971	23 Jul 1971
240	530FX	G-AZMF	British Caledonian Airways	04 Mar 1972	14 Mar 1972
241	476FM	OB-R-1080	Faucett Airways	07 Jul 1971	19 Jul 1974
242	531FS	TI-1095C	LACSA	17 Oct 1972	06 Nov 1972
243	481FW	7Q-YKF	Air Malawi	20 Jan 1972	23 Feb 1972
244	531FS	TI-1096C	LACSA	11 May 1973	14 May 1973
245	479FU	DQ-FBQ	Air Pacific	08 Feb 1972	04 Mar 1972
246	527FK	RP-C1182	Philippine Airlines	01 Jun 1974	14 Jun 1974
247	485GD	1001	Sultan of Oman Air Force	21 Nov 1974	28 Dec 1974
248	527FK	RP-C1183	Philippine Airlines	29 Jun 1974	05 Jul 1974
249	485GD	1002	Sultan of Oman Air Force	20 Dec 1974	29 Jan 1975
250	479FU	DQ-FBV	Air Pacific	16 Jul 1973	04 Aug 1973
251	485GD	1003	Sultan of Oman Air Force	19 Mar 1975	01 Nov 1975
252	525FT	YR-BCI	Tarom	20 Dec 1976	21 Mar 1977
253	525FT	YR-BCJ	Tarom	17 Mar 1977	04 Apr 1977
254	525FT	YR-BCK	Tarom	28 Apr 1977	14 May 1977
255	525FT	YR-BCL	Tarom	17 Jun 1977	09 Jul 1977
256	525FT	YR-BCM	Tarom	08 Aug 1977	25 Aug 1977
257	537GF	5B-DAG	Cyprus Airways	16 Nov 1977	08 Dec 1977
258	537GF	5B-DAH	Cyprus Airways	18 Jan 1978	28 Jan 1978
259	488GH	HZ-MAM	Mouffak Al Midani	28 Apr 1978	19 May 1978

Construction number	Series	Initial	First operator registration	Date of first flight	Date of delivery
260	492GM	G-BLHD	McAlpine Aviation	01 May 1984	09 Jul 1984
261	537GF	5B-DAJ	Cyprus Airways	28 Sept 1978	06 Oct 1978
262	492GM	G-BLDH	McAlpine Aviation	02 Feb 1984	09 Jul 1984
263	539GL	G-BGKE	British Airways	26 Jan 1980	03 Mar 1980
264	539GL	G-BGKF	British Airways	09 May 1980	13 Jun 1980
265	539GL	G-BGKG	British Airways	06 Aug 1980	18 Aug 1980
266	525FT	YR-BCN	Tarom	13 Nov 1980	16 Jan 1981
267	487GK	YR-BCR	Tarom	26 Jun 1981	28 Jul 1981
272	525FT	YR-BCO	Tarom	15 Feb 1982	20 Mar 1982
401	561RC	YR-BRA	Tarom	18 Sept 1982	24 Dec 1982
402	561RC	YR-BRB	Tarom	28 Apr 1983	Jul 1983
403	561RC	YR-BRC	Tarom	26 Apr 1984	Aug 1984
404	561RC	YR-BRD	Tarom	02 Apr 1985	Feb 1986
405	561RC	YR-BRE	Tarom	27 Mar 1986	unknown
406	561RC	YR-BRF	Tarom	30 Sept 1986	unknown
407	561RC	YR-BRG	Tarom	21 Mar 1988	unknown
408	561RC	YR-BRH	Tarom	01 Dec 1988	Mar 1989
409	561RC	YR-BRI	Romavia	03 Oct 1989	unknown
410	497	n/a	unfinished	n/a	n/a
411	561RC	n/a	unfinished	n/a	n/a

The following airframes were assembled at Weybridge:

Construction numbers
033, 034, 083, 084, 091, 096, 158, 159,
160, 163, 165, 168, 183
021–028: Cancelled order for Western Airways.
036–038: Cancelled order for Bonanza Airlines.
047–048: Cancelled order for Western Airways.
095 Reserved for G-ASVT for rebuild of 006 but rebuild cancelled.
164; 169–173; 216–225: not built.
268–271; 273–277: completed in Romania as 401–409.
410–411: partially built in Romania, fate unknown.

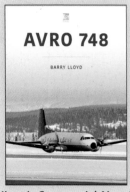

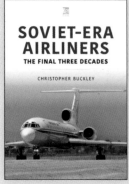